Gayla Trail

Easy Growing

Organic Herbs and Edible Flowers from Small Spaces

Clarkson Potter/Publishers
New York

Library of Congress Cataloging-in-Publication Data
is available upon request.

ISBN 978-0-307-88687-3
eISBN 978-0-307-95325-4

Printed in China

Design by Fluffco
Cover design by Fluffco
Cover photographs by Davin Risk
and Gayla Trail

10 9 8 7 6 5 4 3 2 1

First Edition

To Mr. Barry Parker,
whose lessons about gardening,
life, and friendship have changed
me for the better.

Easy Growing

Contents

Introduction

I have very fond memories of my first herb plant, a little curly parsley that I grew from seed in a foam cup. I was five. It was also my very first plant ever and the gateway to an experience I've spent my adult life repeating over and over again.

I do not recollect actually planting the seed, but I do remember waking up with excitement each morning to see what new magic the little plant had performed overnight. I remember gently rubbing its crinkly green leaves and sneaking ever-so-tiny tastes. The urge to touch, smell, taste, and explore the plant with all of my senses was strong— thankfully it was edible!

In my adult life, gardening with herbs and edible flowers grew out of a desire to make my small rooftop garden as productive and beautiful as possible. Regular, non-edible flowers are nice enough and serve a useful purpose in attracting pollinators and delighting our eyes, but I wanted to fill the empty spots in the tomato and pepper pots with something I could eat. The next thing I knew I was growing thirteen different varieties of basil and seeking out weirdly wonderful herbs with intriguing flavor descriptions that hail from around the world. I had to try them all! I'm still working on it.

Through this exercise in the economy of growing space, I have come to appreciate edible flowers as something more than a sprinkling of potpourri on my plate and have discovered captivating culinary oddities like borage, a pretty blue flower that tastes just like cucumber; Cuban oregano, an indestructible houseplant that tastes like a more potent form of the oregano we're used to; and 'Purple' shiso, a frilly Asian herb that can be brewed into a refreshingly fruity, nuclear pink iced tea.

Herbs may be able to teach us about each other's cuisines, cultures, and histories. Yet at their core they are humble, unpretentious plants, many of which started out as weeds. They're simple to grow and they'll fit into literally any space you can provide them, including but not limited to a crack in a broken patio stone, the step next to your front door, or your bathroom's keyhole windowsill.

Let me show you how.

About This Book

Can I grow herbs on a shady balcony? When do I plant basil? What should I do with a basket of rose petals? Starting a new garden and growing new plants inevitably raises an excess of questions. I wrote this book for all of you new gardeners who are overwhelmed with decisions and have a burning desire to put your own homegrown culinary herbs on the table.

Section One of this book, "Growing an Herb Garden," will walk you through all of the steps involved in growing a healthy, organic herb garden in a myriad of challenging environments. Section Two, "The Plants," will introduce you to more than 200 varieties of herbs and edible flowers, and Section Three, "Keeping Stock: Gather, Preserve, Eat," will be your guide through the processes of harvesting, preserving, and storing your garden's rewards. With easy, DIY projects, recipes, home preserving techniques, and preparation instruction, you'll be well on your way to building an enviable year-round herb pantry.

I also wrote this book for people like me who are already passionate about growing herbs and who want to dive in, try something new, and be wowed. Our eyes are too often larger than our gardening space. I've packed this book full of unusual edible flowers and herbs, and in Section Two, "The Plants," you will also find specific techniques and tricks for growing in pots.

I hope flipping through the pages of this book will inspire an all-new or renewed enthusiasm for your garden and kitchen, as well as motivate you to try new culinary experiences well after the growing season is done.

About the Projects and Recipes

Each project is rated with a difficulty score from 1 to 5 (♦♦♦♦♦) so you can get an idea of the commitment required to make, build, or grow it at a glance.

I've included a range of recipes throughout this book—from savory delights to sweet treats and tasty beverages (alcoholic and not)—as encouragement to use herbs in new ways. Because growing your own allows access to parts of the plants that are not often offered in stores, uses for all edible elements, such as flowers, roots, and seeds, are included. You'll be surprised to discover a delicacy or two growing right under your nose.

It is my hope that flavor variations at the bottom of forty-eight recipes and the sidebars with other herbal substitutions will encourage you to experiment with preferred flavors, take a few risks, and get more mileage out of the plants you are growing in your own garden.

GROWING AN HERB GARDEN

CHAPTER 1

The Pleasure of Herbs and Edible Flowers

Herbs are tactile plants that activate all of our senses, inviting us to touch, smell, and taste them. This is their enchantment. With few exceptions, they are beautiful, ornamental, and elegant in their own right. Their beauty extends from the garden to our plates—herbs make our food come alive and taste better. They inspire new culinary adventures and daydreams.

They make us happy.

Herbs for Everyone

Anyone can grow at least one herb plant. No matter where you live or how much money you have in your wallet, there is an herb for you. One you'll like, too! Herbs are the perfect plants for small-space gardeners who want to grow some of their own food, or for anyone who loves good food and wants more of it. If you have even the smallest inkling that you'd like to try to grow an herb, you should!

On the whole, most culinary herbs and edible flowers are a joy and a delight no matter what sort of growing conditions you're starting with; thankfully, persnickety varieties—or botanical brats—are rare. Barring giants like angelica, borage, and lovage that practically require an estate to accommodate their girth, most stay relatively small or can be trained to stay that way. They are by and large tolerant plants that thrive in cramped quarters and are forgiving enough to put up with trial and error and occasional neglect.

With the exception of rare and foreign varieties, common culinary herbs are affordable to grow if you use your imagination and know where to find cheap plants. Just a few examples:

- Plastic buckets, discarded olive oil cans, and wooden crates make good containers and are free for the taking from the curbside.
- Use thrift store cutlery as digging tools.
- Anything that will hold water can serve as a watering can in a pinch.
- A pack of seeds is cheaper than transplants and offers a heck of a lot more mileage (pages 62–67).
- Split the cost of a plant with a friend and cut it up to make several more (pages 68–69).

Who needs a yard when all it takes to grow an enviable crop of basil is a big pot and a spot of sunshine?

Why Grow Your Own?

Because you're reading this book, chances are that you've got an interest in growing herbs and your own reasons for doing so. If you're not already convinced, the following should seal the deal.

Easy Growing

Herbs are generally undemanding plants that are less susceptible to pests and disease and rarely require special attention to grow lush and productive. For this reason, they are much easier to grow organically than tomatoes or potatoes and are more cost effective to boot. A single pot of basil is prolific, adding sparkle to dozens of summertime meals and a few winter meals, too.

Know What You Grow

Cultivating your own herbs organically ensures that there was nothing on, in, or around them during the growing process that you'd rather not ingest.

Fresh Is Best

Like tomatoes, carrots, and peas, store-bought herbs, even those from the best stores and markets, can't hold a candle to a homegrown herb that has gone directly from your garden to the plate.

Natural Essence

Your homegrown herbs were cultivated outside, basking in the heat and warmth of the sun. The potency of their aromatic, volatile oils is the direct result of this basic, natural alchemy. Herbs that have spent their lives in a greenhouse under artificial lights are a nice midwinter substitute, but a poor imitation for what you can achieve in a pot stuck outside your front door.

Pretty Delicious

Most herbs are as beautiful as they are useful. There is no need to sacrifice aesthetics for the sake of a practical, useful garden. In fact, you may already have an herb or two tucked in among the delphiniums and the daffodils right now, moonlighting as an ornamental. With an herb garden you can indeed have it all, and eat it, too.

Quick Results

Unlike many of our favorite vegetables and fruits that require three months to several years to get to a harvest, many herbs get to their first feast within a month or even a few weeks of planting. And they'll keep producing, too. Some live through just one season; others keep coming back every year like a Rolling Stones tour. Your patience is not required.

Convenience Food

Look, it takes some doing to keep an herb garden alive and thriving, but it is still easier than going all the way to the store to buy a bundle. An herb garden offers months of convenience and mealtime spontaneity. Whenever I can avoid a trip to the grocery store by choosing my seasonings at whim from my own garden, I have more time to laze about with a good book. Enough said.

Have It All

Herbs are certainly gaining a regular place in even the most basic grocery stores, and farmers' markets are catering more and more to a growing demand for the unusual and exotic. Even still, there are all sorts of flowers, roots, seeds, and other delectable plant parts that are too temperamental to find their way to the most sophisticated market stand or gourmet food shop. As a gardener, you have direct access to these seasonal morsels. Lucky you!

The compact size of 'Blue Boy' rosemary makes it the perfect choice for small pots and cramped spaces where nothing else will fit, including balcony ledges and indoors on windowsills.

CHAPTER 2

Creating an Herb Garden Anywhere

It's critical whenever you start a new garden to understand the kind of growing conditions you can or can't provide. Before buying plants or launching a plan for backyard domination, take some time to familiarize yourself with the lay of the land . . . or decking, patio stones, or whatever you've got underfoot. The garden isn't just about the plants that are in the ground; all of the space below and above the soil plays a role in the ecosystem you are about to create.

Location, Location, Location

The following key factors will affect how and what you plant, and whether your plants will flourish or die:

Airflow

Herbs thrive in conditions where the air moves quietly through the space. Gentle breezes that move all around and through the plants can actually toughen them up a bit, while the absence of airflow can lead to powdery mildew and other fungal diseases. High winds, on the other hand, can break stems, stress plants out, and dry out the soil. Urban gardens that are high in the sky with too much or not enough shelter are especially prone to these problems.

Heat

Extreme heat is another urban condition. Tall glass office towers cast shadows, but they also act like gigantic mirrors, radiating a profound amount of heat onto your balcony or yard. Take stock of everything in and around your garden; even the smallest, overlooked details have the potential to create pockets of heat with or without a lot of sun.

Sunlight

Speaking of sun: most herbs need lots of it. Buildings, trees, fences, walls, sheds, garages, and your neighbor's collection of kitschy statuary can block light out of your garden for short or long periods of time throughout the day. Get to know how long and how intensely the sun hits your plants so you can be sure that they are getting what they need.

Plants That Prefer Partial Shade

The following plants prefer partial shade (4–6 hours of direct sun) and will thrive under low-light conditions.

BLOODY DOCK (*Rumex sanguineus*)

LEMON BALM (*Melissa officinalis*)

PANSY AND VIOLA (*Viola* spp.)

SORREL (*Rumex acetosa*)

SWEET CICELY (*Myrrhis odorata*)

SWEET WOODRUFF (*Galium odoratum*)

VIOLET (*Viola odorata*)

WATERCRESS (*Nasturtium officinale*)

WOOD GARLIC (*Allium ursinum*)

Plants That Will Tolerate Partial Shade

These plants will tolerate partial shade, although they may be smaller, less productive, and less healthy over the long term.

ALPINE AND WILD STRAWBERRIES (*Fragaria* spp.)

ANGELICA (*Angelica archangelica*)

ANISE HYSSOP (*Agastache foeniculum*)

CHERVIL (*Anthriscus cerefolium*)

CHIVES (*Allium schoenoprasum*)

CRESS (*Lepidium sativum*)

GARLIC CHIVES (*Allium tuberosum*)

MINT (*Mentha* spp.)

MARJORAM (*Origanum majorana*)

OREGANO (*Origanum vulgare*)

PARSLEY (*Petroselinum crispum*)

SALAD BURNET (*Sanguisorba minor*)

SALAD GREENS

SOCIETY GARLIC (*Tulbaghia violacea*)

THYME (*Thymus* spp.)

From top: Salad greens, violet (*Viola odorata*), and sweet cicely (*Myrrhis odorata*) are just three herbs that will produce a healthy crop when full sun is not available.

Growing in the Ground

Fortunately, herbs are not root vegetables that grow misshapen in rocky, lumpy soil, and they are not broccoli that won't grow a crop worth a damn if the soil is poor. In fact, most of the culinary herbs you're likely to grow will turn into an overgrown, tangled mess if you go to the trouble of piling on endless bags of compost and manure. It's simply more fertilizer than they can handle.

That's not to say that the soil isn't important or that you can just plop a few plants into any old dusty patch of dirt and you're good to go. An organic garden stands on the foundation of healthy, living soil that is teeming with microscopic organisms, wriggling wormy things, good bacteria, and fungi. Keeping chemicals out of there is one way to encourage dead earth to come alive. So is putting back the nutrients your plants remove through annual and biannual doses of homemade compost. See Fertilizing for further instruction (page 44).

Improve Drainage

Roots need air to breathe below the ground or they will rot and eventually die. Healthy soil is full of air. Soil constituents such as sand, clay, organic matter, and so on contribute to how much air there is in the soil, as do the worms and tiny organisms that scurry around in it creating tunnels and tiny holes. Sandy, gritty, or loamy soil that is loose, light, and free draining is ideal for herbs, while densely compacted or clay soils are the worst. The best way to counteract and improve these conditions is to work compost, sand, and grit into the soil over time. Few herbs will thrive in a permanent puddle, although there are a few listed on page 43 that don't mind soggy roots.

Raise It Up

Many urban spaces have compacted soil where there was once concrete, pavement, or heavy foot traffic. It is also common to inherit soil that may be contaminated by old paint chips, or cat and dog feces. A raised bed, or a series of them built above the soil line, is a quick fix for these and a multitude of other sins including compaction, poor drainage, and uneven or sloping yards. Add a layer of gravel at the bottom of the bed to improve drainage, and fill it with soil that is exactly right for the plants you want to grow.

Herbs That Tolerate Poor Soil
Amaranth
Arugula
Borage
Chamomile
Chili Peppers
Coriander
Dill
Fennel
Lavender
'Lemon Mint' Marigold
Marjoram
Nasturtium
Oregano
Purslane
Sage
Thyme

Grow a Gravel Garden

If you plan to focus on Mediterranean plants such as lavender and sage that prefer nutritionally poor soil that is dry and hot, you can skip the hard work of improving drainage and make your garden bed out of gravel instead. Lay a deep layer of gravel on top of the old soil, dump in a bit of compost for nutrition, and plant right into that. Easy peasy.

Nitty Gritty

A little bit of sand, grit, or gravel in the bottom of a planting hole can help fix minor emergencies when the soil drainage is poor. A thinner layer of pea gravel laid on top of the garden as a mulch is another way to improve drainage. It will also keep weeds down, prevent backsplash when you water, and heat up the soil. It's great for pots, too.

Miniature Raised Bed

Make It

A large raised bed is a good way out of the backbreaking work required to improve large areas of very badly compacted or generally lousy soil. But in smaller areas when only a few plants need special treatment, an old dresser drawer can stand in as a temporary, miniature version.

1. Using a hammer, jigsaw, or any other tools that may be required, knock, bang, or cut the bottom out of an old dresser drawer or crate. Drill lots of holes for drainage if you can't remove it entirely.

2. Dig a shallow hole that is slightly wider than the bottomless box, set the box in the hole, and fill the box up with soil, sand, gravel, compost, or other amendments.

3. Plant it up!

TIP: To keep slugs out of raised beds, wrap a strip of copper tape all around the top edge of the box. It acts like an electric fence to repel these slimy pests from parsley, pansies, and the other herbs and flowers they love to eat.

Growing in Containers

A container garden is not a lesser version of the real thing. A container garden is a real garden; all of the joys and occasional tears are simply held inside pots rather than in the earth.

Most herbs take to containers rather well, sometimes better than in the ground. Because you are creating your plants' living foundation from scratch, you control the quality of the soil and drainage, the amount of water they receive and when, sun exposure, and location. Pots are also an easy solution for tender herbs that go indoors for the winter. They offer easy mobility and the chance to change things up when a plant is not working out, or simply as the mood takes you.

It's All in the Pot

- Plants like parsley that grow deep roots need a deep container to stretch out in.
- Tall plants like dill and fennel are better off in a pot that has some girth to prevent them from falling over in the wind.
- Sage, rosemary, and other herbs that like good drainage grow best in tall "rose pots" that are narrower at the bottom than the top. The slanting, tapered shape draws water down and out the bottom easily so that the roots are never sitting in soggy soil.
- Wide, stout pots with straight sides are best for crawling plants like creeping savory or thyme that have a shallow, weblike root system.

True Grit

Remember, most herbs thrive in soil with exceptional drainage. Add sand or grit to regular potting soil, but if you can't find either, mix 1 part potting soil to $1\frac{1}{2}$ parts cactus soil.

Set It and Forget It

For herbs that like their soil constantly moist, such as nasturtiums, watercress, and sorrel, self-watering containers offer a helping hand and are especially invaluable to rooftop or urban gardeners when the midsummer heat kicks into overdrive. Unfortunately, these systems aren't always suitable, because most herbs need to dry out ever so slightly in between waterings.

Use vertical space and create a sense of height by displaying pots on the steps of an old kitchen stool.

To promote good drainage, drill one ¼–½" hole into the bottom of the pot for every inch or two of pot width.

No Holes Barred

Literally anything that holds soil can be a container. Let your creativity run wild. However, drainage holes are an absolute must—no *if*s, *and*s, or *but*s. Garden shops sell pots without them, but take it from me: no herb will survive for any length of time without adequate drainage, no matter how much gravel you put in before planting. Make lots of holes in the bottom of cooking pots, thrift-store pottery, wooden crates, or anything else that doesn't have them already (at least one ¼" hole, every 2 inches). A drill fitted with a masonry bit works on pottery, and an oversized carpentry nail and hammer can punch holes in metal.

Place a square of thin tissue paper, used window screening, or landscape cloth over holes that are too big to hold soil in. Line open-weave baskets, hats, crates, and other items that won't hold soil with landscape cloth, sheets made of coir, or plastic bags with holes punched in them for drainage.

Let It Flow

Avoid the use of drip trays when possible, especially in the spring when there is a lot of rain. Plants that are left sitting in water for long periods of time run the risk of rotting. Moisture-dependent plants like watercress and lemongrass are the exception. Prop plants like rosemary and lavender that require good drainage on top of bricks to improve the flow of water out the bottom of the pot. Alternatively, line drip trays with pebbles or gravel so that the pot is sitting above the waterline.

Mulch

Mulch the top of your pots with grit, used aquarium gravel, beach glass, small pebbles, or terra-cotta balls. They warm up the soil, improve drainage, and give your pots a slick finish. Mulch parsley, chervil, sorrel, and other plants that prefer cool, moist soil with straw, cocoa shells, or buckwheat hulls instead.

Supersize It

Large containers that are 18″ deep or more are easier to care for than small pots because they don't dry out as easily, and the roots have lots of room to grow into.

If you have to stay small, stick with herbs that have shallow root systems and don't mind cramped quarters or a bit of drought. Coriander, cress, thyme, violas, Cuban oregano, 'Apple' or 'Nutmeg' geranium, and chives are all good contenders for small pots.

Mixed Planters: 5 Aesthetically Pleasing Combinations for Window Boxes and Large Pots

- VINTAGE COAL BUCKET: Parsley, thyme, basil, rosemary, summer savory, and French sorrel, page 7.
- IT WAS ALL YELLOW: A gold and pastel theme in a wooden crate: lemon thyme, 'Creamsicle' nasturtium, 'Golden' marjoram, violas, and 'Fish' chili pepper, page 2.
- SPRING HERBS: Colorful chive blossoms, variegated 'Silver' thyme, and purple violas in a large metal basin, page 11.
- EVERYDAY EATING: Basil, French tarragon, and summer savory, page 39.
- WINDOW BOX: Creeping savory, violas, variegated oregano, see right.

Tiered Herb Pot Tower

Make It

A tower of pots is a creative way to grow a lot of herbs using vertical space. It works just like a strawberry pot, but instead of cramped and shallow pockets, each herb has ample root space to grow into. It's a lot easier to maintain and plant up, too!

You Will Need

1 small terra-cotta pot (5" tall, 6" wide top, 3½" wide bottom)

1 medium terra-cotta pot (6" tall, 8" wide top, 5" wide bottom)

1 large terra-cotta pot (11" × 5")

Potting soil

4" pot 'Tricolor' sage

4" pot 'Golden' oregano

4" pot 'Caraway' thyme

4" pot Roman chamomile

Drainage tray (optional)

Choosing Containers

I've included the exact pot sizes I used to build the layered pot depicted here; of course, other pot sizes will work well, too. Choose a bottom pot that is super wide and a pot for the middle layer with a bottom that is about half the size of the bottom pot. This will ensure that the plants on the bottom layer get the most growing space possible. Follow this equation for the top layer, but try not to go any smaller than 4–5" wide. You'll be hard-pressed to find an herb that will happily grow in less space than that.

It should go without saying that all pots must have drainage holes.

Choosing Plants

Use your imagination to come up with your own planting combinations. Select a few draping plants such as creeping savory, 'Lemon Gem' marigold, or thyme that will soften the edges of the tower and a few upright plants (basil, sage, or rosemary) to create contrasting height.

Try to match the number and type of plants to the size of the pots you use. For example, a combination of pots that are equal in size to the one shown opposite works best with plants that stay relatively small and aren't fussy about root space and depth. Thyme plants tend to work best on top where they get a lot of light and the soil dries out quickly.

Don't go overboard cramming plants in at planting time. They'll fill out the pot in no time and will be happiest with a bit of room to stretch out and grow.

1. Fill the large and medium containers with potting soil to within an inch of the top.

2. Set the medium pot on top of the soil of the bottom pot, pushing it toward the very edge of the back so that there is as much room in front as possible. Press the medium pot into the soil a little bit to steady it.

3. Now scoop some soil out of the bottom pot until there is enough space to plant the 'Tricolor' sage and the 'Golden' oregano. Add some soil back in around the plants, pressing it in so that there is still an inch of space between the soil line and the top of the pot.

4. Pot up the third, smallest pot with 'Caraway' thyme, again maintaining an inch of space between the soil and the top edge of the container.

5. Press the small pot into the middle pot as you did in step 2. Scoop some soil out of the middle pot and plant in the Roman chamomile and 'Purple Bush' basil.

6. Water all three pots until water starts to drip out from their drainage holes. Carefully place the tower in a sunny spot with a wall or fence behind it for extra support.

Variations

Don't be afraid to try unusual pots made of different materials. You can even try moving the positioning of the stacked containers around by alternating sides. Prop a wooden crate diagonally across the corner of another similarly sized crate using the edges for support instead of the soil. Stack smaller squares inside larger squares.

CHAPTER 3

Making It Pretty

Designing a new garden, especially your first one ever, can be incredibly exciting, but it's also a process. An empty patch of soil is like a blank canvas, full of possibility and potential, and sometimes a source of fear. The question of where to begin and the internal anxiety to make it pretty and then keep it alive has stopped a lot of would-be gardeners before they've even started. It helps to think of gardening as a kind of serious, adult play. After all, you're messing about with dirt!

Most of us start out small with a basic idea that shifts and changes as plants come to us piecemeal from here and there over weeks, months, even years. The time it takes may seem like a disadvantage, but building a culinary herb garden in stages leaves room for it to evolve with you as you gain experience growing and cooking with new herbs.

Of course, things can go wrong under the best conditions. Plants die from neglect, disease, and pests, and for a million other reasons. Others just don't thrive where we put them even when the tag says they should. There are some mysteries in the garden that even so-called experts don't always understand. It's also not uncommon for beginners to miscalculate the mature size and girth of immature transplants. Angelica, as an example, is no bigger than parsley when you bring it home from the store, but can grow into an 8-foot-tall behemoth in its second year. You can move it, but that may require a crane.

Fortunately, no garden is permanent. You can always change your mind and relocate a plant that isn't working, or dig the whole garden up and start again. One of the greatest challenges and joys in gardening is that you can tinker with layout and design to your heart's content. It's not quite as simple as moving a chair or rearranging the living room, but it can be done with very little harm to the plants. And even if a few plants do die along the way, so what? It doesn't make you a bad person, or even a bad gardener. The road to building a gorgeous garden is lined with legions of dead plants, some of which we didn't even like anyway. Vacancies are an open invitation to put in something better.

Adding Herbs to a Garden

If starting from scratch is too tall an order or space is at a premium, why not ease your way into herb gardening by introducing a handful of plants to a preexisting ornamental bed? There is no rule that says you must create a dedicated herb garden or keep herbs and ornamentals separated. The vast majority of culinary herbs and flowers are gorgeous in their own right—the only difference is that they are edible, too.

Grow your own miniature lavender farm by piling the soil in long mounds with walking spaces in between. This growing style makes a dramatic visual impact, and the plants benefit from the good drainage and soil warmth it offers.

Designing the Herb Garden

If you've got space and sun, the sky is the limit. There are so many culinary herbs and flowers to choose from, you could cut out every other type of plant for the rest of your life and never be at a loss for something new and intriguing to try.

An herb garden is less restricted than other sorts of edible gardens and offers a greater opportunity to play with design. Unlike fruit-bearing vegetables that tend to be in their prime for only a short period of time, most herb plants look beautiful at several stages throughout the season, and many look as good without flowers as they do with them.

A garden can be rigidly structured and formal or totally wild depending on what suits your taste and creative impulse. Of course, not putting a solid plan to paper is a perfectly viable option. It's more important that you truly enjoy your garden than get bent out of shape about the design. Still, some styles are less productive in a small space. For example, growing in orderly rows eats up precious real estate in a postage stamp plot, and packing too much in too tightly may make the space look full at first but can result in a garden of feeble, stunted plants. It helps to have even a vague idea of what you want to accomplish before you start throwing plants into the ground at random. Planning can be fun—it doesn't have to cramp your style or suffocate your sense of adventure.

Breaking It Down

Over the years, I've used a method for dividing up the garden that sits somewhere between orderly and wild. It offers the structure of formalism but is still very adaptable and lends itself to spontaneity and play as you find new plants to try.

Step 1: Partitioning and Edging

To begin, break up a large area or yard into beds fashioned into simple shapes like rectangles and squares. Partitioning the space makes it feel more manageable and less overwhelming than a wide-open expanse.

Edging provides a repetitive visual structure that contains the plants inside it. On a practical level, a hedge or wall holds the soil in place and creates a microclimate by acting as a protective barrier against cold winds, driving rain, and erosion.

Step 2: Laying Down the Path

Herb gardens need paths so that you can walk between the beds and gain easy access for maintenance and picking. Paths are like edging in that they act as a conduit that draws your eyes through the garden.

Formal gardens tend to have very linear, concise paths that lead you in direct lines through the space. Informal gardens make use of winding paths that slow down visual movement, creating blind spots and secret surprises.

PATH MATERIALS

Paths protect plants by directing the flow of traffic off the growing areas. They can also work to keep weeds down. Salvaged bricks and paving stones are long-lasting choices. Mulches such as woodchips and cocoa hulls are affordable and simple, but these organic materials decompose quickly and need to be replenished yearly.

Mix things up by spacing paving stones widely and erratically with thyme planted in between. Black landscape fabric, wood planks, and even plain old cardboard are low-cost path options that don't appear cheap when used with intention and repeated over a large area. Laying pathways and edging beds can be expensive depending on the materials you use, but neither has to happen in the first year. You can always start with more affordable, less permanent materials and replace them in sections over time.

LIVING PATHWAYS

A living pathway composed entirely of tough, walkable thyme varieties such as mother-of-thyme (*Thymus serpyllum*), creeping thyme (*Thymus praecox* 'Coccineus'), and woolly thyme (*Thymus pseudolanuginosus*) or fragrant chamomile (*Chamaemelum nobile* and *Chamaemelum nobile* 'Treneague') is a stunning option that is lovely with a border of lavender or rosemary.

Edging Materials
Bent bamboo poles

Bricks

Cedar planks
(naturally rot-resistant)

Cement blocks (plant in the holes, too)

Large rocks

Logs

Metal strips

Recycled wood

Woven twig fence

Living Hedges
Boxwood

Lavender

Lemon verbena

Rosemary

Rugosa roses

Pathway Materials

Enduring
Bricks

Gravel

Paving stones
(Homemade or prefab)

River rocks

Tumbled glass

Wood planks

Temporary
Buckwheat

Cardboard

Cocoa hulls

Straw

Wood chips

Step 3: Choosing a Design

Next, divide the bed or beds up further by arranging smaller shapes inside like puzzle pieces. Choose squares and diamonds arranged in an orderly fashion if you're striving for a sense of uniformity and formality. Toss in odd shapes and curves for a softer, wilder look. Pies, pinwheels, spirals, and knots are also commonly used shapes for herb gardens.

Step 4: Filling It In

Fill in the spaces according to their size and the growth habits of the chosen plants. Fill small shapes with one large plant that will reach its edges, or several of one type of small plant. Growing in dense groupings of the same plant looks full and eye-catching, especially when they're in bloom.

This also works if you grow several similar plants of different varieties together. For example, organize your garden by type with all of the basils together in one or more quadrants, and oregano and marjoram in another. Break it down further by growth habit—even when the leaf colors are different, the repetition of height and growing style creates uniformity and tones down the chaos.

How Many Plants Do I Need?

If growing food is your primary concern, don't forget to consider the harvest size each plant will provide. I can say from personal experience that an entire bed of sage is stunning to behold, but a single mature plant will produce more sage than a reality television family can eat in a lifetime. Fill the largest spaces up with herbs you enjoy cooking with and you'll get the best of both worlds.

Tall Herbs

You can count on the following herbs and edible flowers to grow 3 feet or taller for eye-catching drama.

- Amaranth (some types)
- Angelica (*Angelica* spp.)
- Bay (*Laurus nobilis*)
- Dill 'Mammoth' (*Anethum graveolens*)
- Elderberry (*Sambucus* spp.)
- Fennel (*Foeniculum vulgare*)
- Fuchsia (*Fuchsia* subsp.)
- Hollyhock (*Alcea rosea*)
- Lemon verbena (*Aloysia triphylla*)
- Lilac (*Syringa vulgaris*)
- Mexican oregano (*Lippia graveolens*)
- Redbud (*Cercis canadensis*)
- Safflower (*Carthamus tinctorius*)
- Sunflower (*Helianthus annuus*)
- Sweet cicely (*Myrrhis odorata*)

Climbing Herbs

Beautify a bare fence, wall, or arbor with these vigorous (and fabulous) vines.

- Fava bean (*Vicia faba*)
- Honeysuckle (*Lonicera japonica*)
- Hops (*Humulus lupulus*)
- Jasmine (*Jasminum officinale*)
- Pea (*Pisum sativum*)
- Rose (climbers)
- Runner bean (*Phaseolus coccineus*)

Carpeting and Ground Cover

These creeping plants stay very low to the ground and make a soft and sprawling living carpet underneath tall and climbing herbs.

- English chamomile (*Chamaemelum nobile* 'Treneague')
- Purslane (*Portulaca oleracea*)
- Roman chamomile (*Chamaemelum nobile*)
- Thyme (*Thymus* spp.)
- Wild arugula (*Diplotaxis tenuifolia*)

Choosing the Plants

Here are a few things to consider when placing plants in your garden:

Height and Spread

The most common arrangement is tall or climbing plants and objects in the back, gradating to midsized bushes and plants in the middle and short plants and sprawling carpets in front. In the case of gardens without a back wall, the tallest height is generally in the center of the bed, gradually decreasing to the edges. Of course, you don't have to be so exacting. Playing with where you position height can move the eye around the garden in a more natural, free-flowing way. Don't forget to consider the shade cast by tall plants; underplant them with herbs that prefer the protection of an overhanging canopy.

Color

The colors we use in the rooms of our home help create an overall atmosphere—and the same can be applied to the garden. The planter's palette is as varied as a box of paints; use the following to create a mood that suits your sense of style.

- A plan based on a monochromatic or single color scheme is the simplest beginner's approach to garden design (shown in both photos above).
- Use foliage, texture, and size to break up what could be an otherwise flat look.
- Another simple option is to choose combinations that are close to one another: green-blue and blue, violet and blue, yellow and orange, red-orange and orange, and so on.
- Pairing contrasting colors is bold and eye-popping, but borders on blinding if you're not careful. The contrast of a white-and-green leaf next to a dark one, for instance, is startling. One way to avoid overkill is to tone down one plant and ramp up the other. Grow a smaller clump of the brighter color next to a field of the other. Pair a small but vibrant plant with a large and subdued one, or contrast plants with differing leaf sizes.
- By all means, use every single color in the rainbow if that makes you happy. They have a fancy name for that, too: polychromatic color scheme (aka crazy plant lady).

Foliage

Timing when your plants will flower is like choreographing a dance—it's a skill you'll develop over time as you familiarize yourself with the plants you grow. Until you reach that stage, planting according to leaf shape and texture can take you a long way. After all, flowers come and go, but foliage is a constant that you can count on throughout most of the growing season.

Set plants with wildly divergent leaf shapes beside one another, or choose plants with contrasting colors but identical textures. Curly parsley (*Petroselinum crispum*), 'Green Ruffles' and 'Purple Ruffles' basil, 'Prince Rupert' geranium, purple shiso, and bloody dock (above left) are just a few examples of herbs with crinkly, coiled, and twisted forms.

The leaves of lemon verbena and common garden sage are rough like a cat's tongue. The 'Berggarten' variety has a soft and rounded shape that is even prettier. Spiky dianthus looks intriguing set against a field of low-growing thyme (above right). Angelica, lovage, fennel, and dill are architectural giants that make a statement on their own.

Trailing rosemary varieties including 'Santa Barbara' and 'Blue Boy' shape themselves into exciting bonsai-like forms with absolutely no effort on your part. Fennel, chervil, and Fernleaf geranium (*Pelargonium denticulatum* 'Filicifolium') have delicate, bobbing foliage that works next to simple, rounded leaf shapes.

Leaf Shapes and Textures

Soft/Furry

'Apple Scented' geranium (*Pelargonium odoratissimum*)

Borage (*Borago officinalis*)

Lavender (*Lavandula* spp.)

Nutmeg geranium (*Pelargonium fragrans*)

'Peppermint' geranium (*Pelargonium tomentosum*)

Woolly thyme (*Thymus pseudolanuginosus*)

Spiky/Elongated

Chives (*Allium schoenoprasum*)

Clove pinks (*Dianthus* spp.)

Egyptian walking onion (*Allium cepa* var. *proliferum*)

Elephant garlic (*Allium ampeloprasum*)

French tarragon (*Artemisia dracunculus*)

Garlic chives (*Allium tuberosum*)

Ginger (*Zingiber officinale*)

Leeks (*Allium ampeloprasum* Porrum Group)

Lemongrass (*Cymbopogon citratus*)

Rosemary (*Rosmarinus officinalis*)

Savory (*Satureja* spp.)

Ferny/Serrated

Chervil (*Anthriscus cerefolium*)

Fennel (*Foeniculum vulgare*)

Lovage (*Levisticum officinale*)

Marigold Gem Series (*Tagetes tenuifolia*)

Marigold 'Signet' (*Tagetes tenuifolia*)

Roman chamomile (*Chamaemelum nobile*)

Salad burnet (*Sanguisorba minor*)

Sweet cicely (*Myrrhis odorata*)

Wormwood (*Artemisia absinthium*)

Round/Curvaceous

French sorrel (*Rumex scutatus*)

Nasturtium (*Tropaeolum majus*)

Purslane (*Portulaca oleracea*)

Sage 'Berggarten'

Crinkly/Curly

Basil 'Green Ruffles'

Basil 'Napoletano'

Basil 'Purple Ruffles'

Curly mint (*Mentha spicata* var. *crispum*)

Curly parsley (*Petroselinum crispum*)

Lemon-scented geranium (*Pelargonium crispum* × 'Prince Rupert')

Oregano 'Golden'

Shiso (*Perilla frutescens*)

Rough

Anise hyssop (*Agastache foeniculum*)

Basil 'African Blue'

Basil, Tulsi (*Ocimum tenuiflorum*)

Basil 'West African'

Catmint (*Nepeta* × *faassenii*)

Catnip (*Nepeta cataria*)

Lemon balm (*Melissa officinalis*)

Lemon verbena (*Aloysia triphylla*)

Sage (*Salvia* spp.)

Spearmint

Scented geraniums (*Pelargonium* spp.)

Leaf Colors

Silver/Grey Blue
Catmint (*Nepeta × faassenii*)
Catnip (*Nepeta cataria*)
Clove pinks (*Dianthus* spp.)
Common garden sage (*Salvia officinalis*)
Dittany of Crete (*Origanum dictamnus*)
Lavender (*Lavandula* spp.)
Marjoram (*Origanum majorana*)
Sage (*Salvia* spp.)
Thyme 'Silver' (*Thymus × citriodorus*)

Purple/Black
Basil 'Dark Opal'
Basil 'Osmin'
Basil 'Purple Bush'
Basil 'Purple Delight'
Basil 'Purple Ruffles'
Basil, Purple Tulsi (*Ocimum tenuiflorum*)
Sage 'Purple'

Chartreuse
Anise hyssop 'Golden Jubilee'
Bay 'Aurea'
Golden purslane (*Portulaca oleracea*)
Hops 'Aureus'
Lemon balm 'Golden'
Oregano 'Golden'
Marjoram 'Golden'
Rosemary 'Golden Rain'
Sage 'Golden'
Thyme 'Golden Lemon'

Variegated
Basil 'Perpetual Pesto'
Basil 'Variegated African Blue'
Chocolate mint geranium (*Pelargonium quercifolium* 'Chocolate Mint')
Cuban oregano 'Variegated' (*Plectranthus amboinicus*)
Lady Plymouth geranium (*Pelargonium × asperum*)
Lemon balm 'Aurea'
Logee mint (*Mentha × piperita* 'Logee')
Nasturtium 'Alaska Mix'
Pineapple mint (*Mentha suaveolens* 'Variegata')
Rosemary 'Aureus'
Sage 'Tricolor'
Thyme 'Doone Valley'
Thyme 'Silver Queen'
Variegated mint-rose geranium (*Pelargonium × asperum* 'Variegatum')
Variegated nutmeg geranium (*Pelargonium × fragrans* 'Variegated')
Variegated Prince Rupert geranium (*Pelargonium crispum* × 'Variegated Prince Rupert')

Red/Bronze
Amaranth 'Red Army'
Angelica gigas
Basil 'Red Rubin'
Bronze fennel
Mustard 'Japanese Red Giant'
Purple shiso (*Perilla frutescens*)
Red orache (*Atriplex hortensis*)
Rosa glauca (*Rosa rubrifolia*)

CHAPTER 4

Growing Care

If you think you have a "black thumb," chances are you just haven't met the right plant. Yet. There are countless herbs out there that favor a breadth of growing preferences and an equal number of herb varieties with different flavors to suit a wide range of taste palates. The right plants for you are out there; it just takes a bit of background knowledge to find them.

Choosing Plants

The first thing you'll need to know about your new herb is its name, preferably its formal or botanical name. Marigolds and pot marigolds can mean the same or different plants depending on where you are and whom you're talking to, but if you say Tagetes and Calendula everyone knows exactly what you mean. When it comes to plants that will end up in your mouth, these small, regional distinctions can be literally life or death.

Family connections are equally important because they point to how a plant grows and which plants they should be grown with. Apiaceae or umbellifers (dill, coriander, fennel) tend to prefer well-draining soil and sun, whereas composites or aster family plants (chamomile, sunflowers) are sun worshippers that prefer their soil on the drier side. While there are always exceptions, herbs in the same family generally favor similar growing conditions, so you know you can safely plant them together in the garden and harvest them in the same way.

On the other hand, at times plants from the same families should be kept at a distance because they share the same pests and diseases. As you get familiar with the plants you grow, you'll soon start to notice similarities that will make family identification in the store or out in the field quick and easy. Umbelliferous herbs are known for their umbrella-like flowers. Mint family herbs have square stems, and composite flowers all look like miniature or oversized daisies.

For everyday eating, grow basil, tarragon, and summer savory together in a medium-sized pot like this 12" deep, glazed crock.

Choosing Healthy Plants and Bulbs

Use these guidelines to get the most out of your plant budget at the garden shop. On the whole you get what you pay for, but you can scoop up some good deals if you know what to look out for.

- **ANNUALS VERSUS PERENNIALS:** Only buy annuals that are in tiptop shape and in season, because they will be dead soon anyway. You can save money and buy sale perennials that have gone dormant and are a little worse for wear because they will have lots of time to bounce back.

- **BIG, BUT NOT BETTER:** Choose short and stocky over tall and lanky plants. Unless the size is proportioned, it can mean the plant is straining for light rather than robust.

- **INSECT INVASION:** Quickly scan the plants and the area around the plants for visible signs of the pests listed on pages 52–54. Are fungus gnats or whiteflies buzzing around the pots? Check underneath leaves for aphids and along tree trunks and branches for scale.

- **IT'S IN THE LEAVES:** Unless you are buying off-season, herb foliage should not be yellowing, crispy, or pocked with pits, marks, or soft spots. Err on the side of caution and avoid introducing a new disease to your garden.

- **EARLY BLOOMERS:** Avoid flowering perennials that are blooming ahead of schedule. Stressed-out plants rush to procreate as a last-ditch attempt at keeping the gene pool alive. Flowering bulbs are often forced into early blooming to attract buyers, but the health of the bulb suffers for it.

- **ROOT-BOUND:** Plants that have roots sticking out of the bottom of the drainage holes have been in the pot too long and are under stress for space, nutrients, and water. This can make them poor candidates for transplanting.

- **BUYING BULBS AND ROOTS:** Healthy bulbs and roots are plump and firm with no visible signs of disease. Put them back if they are desiccated, soft, or moldy.

Plants for Your Climate

Hot or cold, your climate doesn't have to limit the herb plants you can grow, but it will overwhelmingly influence how you grow them.

- **Hardy** perennials are the toughest nuts of the bunch. They can withstand winters that dip well below freezing (5°F) and will come back in the spring raring to go.
- **Half-hardy** or **tender** herbs probably won't make it through a killing frost and will have to come indoors for the winter if your region dips below 32°F and stays there.

Plants such as thyme, arugula, variegated sages, and lavender can sit on the fence between hardy and half-hardy—it all depends on the year and your soil. For example, lavender and thyme put up with colder temperatures as long as the soil drains really well. Sometimes all they need is a warming layer of mulch or a protective burlap wrap to keep them alive until spring.

Growing in a Warm Climate

- Watch water levels during the hot, dry season—even drought-tolerant herbs such as lavender have their limit.
- During the hottest months, move potted plants that dry out quickly into the shadow cast by a fence or tree, where they will receive protection from midday sun.
- Plants like hardneck garlic that rely on a long, cold dormant period won't make it in the tropics. In that case you'll want to go in the opposite direction and keep them potted up in the fridge to fake the winter your garden can't provide.

Growing in a Cold Climate

- Be aware of your region's last frost date in the spring and the first frost date in the fall. These dates will determine when it is safe to put tender plants outside and when they need to come back in.
- First and last frost dates are also helpful benchmarks for determining when to get long-season seeds started indoors, and when to start end-of-season crops outdoors (pages 64–65).

Different Strokes

All plants have their own life cycle, which determines how long they'll last in your garden. Knowing the plants' life spans will help you decide how to grow them and whether they need a permanent home or a temporary spot jammed in next to the roses. I have indicated which category each plant in Section Two of this book falls under, so you'll never have to guess.

- **Annuals** never make it past a year, and some even die before the end of one season. Cilantro, fennel, and nasturtiums are great for filling up empty spaces and are usually very easy to grow from seed.
- **Self-seeding annuals** go kaput when their jig is up, but come back and start all over again in the spring via the seeds they drop into the soil. You never have to plant calendula, borage, or dill again; unfortunately, you can't get rid of them either.
- **Biennial** plants survive from the same root for two years tops, making lots of leaves in year one, followed by flowers and seeds in the second year. Lovage and parsley are a few examples.
- **Perennials** flower and set seed yearly, yet they spring forth and prosper from the same root almost indefinitely. Sage, lavender, and a few others tend to lose their luster at around the 3- to 5-year mark and are worth replacing if you want a decent harvest. Oregano, mint, and roses never need replacing. Perennials are more expensive in stores but are worth it for their longevity.

Watering

Good drainage in the herb garden is key. When you water, watch to see whether puddles form or the water disappears quickly. Plants that are waterlogged either are growing in soil that is not draining well or are being overwatered. Adjust the soil drainage (page 19) and how often you water according to the plant's needs.

Most culinary herbs are drought tolerant, but there are a few exceptions to the rule, including lemongrass and sorrel, which prefer soil that's on the moist side. Take a minute to acquaint yourself with the watering needs of each new plant. Section Two of this book serves as a reference guide. It's difficult to moderate the soil moisture of adjoining plants. Match plants up in the garden or in a pot with other herbs that prefer similar conditions. That way the mint won't get too dry and the sage won't get too wet.

Watering Outdoor Plants

- All seedlings—even drought-tolerant plants—should be kept moist through the critical weeks after planting. Once established, cut back the frequency (not the amount) in stages until you reach a point at which the soil dries out slightly in between.
- Water drought-tolerant herbs infrequently, but very thoroughly. Deep watering makes healthier roots that anchor farther down into the soil.
- Water herbs that require consistently wet soil often. You'll have the most luck growing them in low-lying areas of the garden where water tends to puddle and pool.
- Don't skimp on water at planting time. Water in well. Make a moat around each plant, wait until the water has soaked into the soil, and apply again. If roots are thoroughly quenched from the beginning, they will settle into their new environment and grow much faster.
- Water the soil directly and try to avoid spraying the leaves. This is especially critical with bee balm, sage, and other herbs that are susceptible to powdery mildew (see page 55).

Tolerant of Consistently Damp Soil

CHERVIL (*Anthriscus cerefolium*)
FRENCH SORREL (*Rumex scutatus*)
LEMON BALM (*Melissa officinalis*)
LOVAGE (*Levisticum officinale*)
SORREL (*Rumex acetosa*)

Tolerant of Very Wet Soil

BEE BALM (*Monarda didyma*)
BLOODY DOCK (*Rumex sanguineus*)
LEMONGRASS (*Cymbopogon citratus*)
MINT (*Mentha* spp.)
VIOLETS (*Viola odorata*)
WASABI (*Wasabia japonica*)
WATERCRESS (*Nasturtium officinale*)
WATER MINT (*Mentha aquatica*)

Fertilizing

When it comes to fertilizing an herb garden, less is more. Most culinary herbs are not heavy feeders because they are primarily grown for their leaves and seeds. The task they've been assigned is nowhere near as strenuous as the hard work of an 8-foot-high tomato plant or a rambling pumpkin plant. In fact, Mediterranean herbs including rosemary, sage, oregano, and savory become more strongly flavored when they are grown in slightly poor soil; overfertilizing makes them tasteless, soft, and an easy target for insect pests.

A mature in-ground garden that is reasonably fertile may not need much more than a biannual dose of compost and sea kelp fertilizer scratched into the soil surface. Apply Homegrown Liquid Feed (page 46) through the spring and summer when plants are most actively growing. At the store, choose an organic fertilizer mix that is reasonably balanced or one that has a slightly higher nitrogen content.

Fertilizing Tips

- Never fertilize plants that are not actively growing or are about to go into a dormant period. Reduce or completely stop fertilizing during low-light months (winter). Plants will grow leggy and weak without adequate light to support rapid growth stimulated by fertilizers.
- Plants that are heavily harvested have to work hard to replenish with new growth. Feed them a little extra around early to midsummer.
- Add crushed eggshells to the soil around lavender, thyme, oregano, leeks, and rosemary to sweeten the soil.
- Containers are depleted of nutrients faster than in-ground gardens. Apply watered-down liquid fertilizer to container gardens every week or so throughout the growing season.

Organic Fertilizers

SOURCES: Dry fish fertilizer, liquid fish emulsion, sea kelp (aka kelp meal), bonemeal, bloodmeal, greensand, worm castings, chicken manure, alfalfa meal, rock phosphate, cottonseed meal, and bat guano.

HOMEMADE: Compost, vermicompost (worm poo), Homegrown Liquid Feed (page 46), coffee grounds, fish and shellfish scraps, banana peels, and cooled cooking water.

Nutrients and What They Do

If you look closely, your plants will tell you what they are lacking nutritionally. You can also order an analysis from your county's extension office that will tell you exactly where your soil is nutrient rich and where it could use a little help.

Primary Nutrients

Primary nutrients are the most essential to overall plant health. They are needed in high quantities and are most often in short supply in the soil.

Nitrogen (N): Promotes lush, vibrant leaves.

SYMPTOMS OF DEFICIENCY: Older leaves turn yellow and plants grow slowly and stunted.

Phosphorus (P): Responsible for general plant health: root systems, flower and fruit formation.

SYMPTOMS OF DEFICIENCY: Plants grow slowly; leaves turn bluish-green with a purple tint and are undersized. Plants exhibit poor flowering and fruit yields.

Potassium (K): Helps plants recover from periods of stress. Responsible for the movement of materials through the plant (food, water, etc.).

SYMPTOMS OF DEFICIENCY: Plants are frail, spindly, and disease-prone and lack resilience. Leaf tips exhibit yellowing and brown scorching.

Secondary Nutrients

Secondary nutrients are just as essential, but more readily available in the soil. They are the least likely to require supplementing.

Calcium (Ca): Builds and strengthens cell walls. Aids in root development.

SYMPTOMS OF DEFICIENCY: Deficiency is less common in leafy herbs. Blossom-end rot appears on fruit. Young leaves may curl.

Magnesium (Mg): A key component in chlorophyll, making it essential for photosynthesis. Aids in nitrogen fixing and phosphorus uptake.

SYMPTOMS OF DEFICIENCY: Plants exhibit stunted growth and weak stalks. Mature leaves turn yellow with dark green veins, then finally rusty brown.

Sulfur (S): Helps with nitrogen fixing and chlorophyll formation.

SYMPTOMS OF DEFICIENCY: Yellowing of younger leaves persists after nitrogen is added. Plants are stunted and thinner.

Trace Elements and Minerals

Trace elements and minerals are needed in small amounts but should not be overlooked or ignored.

Copper (Cu): Promotes disease resistance, reproductive/seed production, and water regulation.

SYMPTOMS OF DEFICIENCY: Plants exhibit poor growth and inability to flower or reproduce. Leaves curl or drop.

Iron (Fe): A component of chlorophyll.

SYMPTOMS OF DEFICIENCY: New growth turns yellow or white. Veins are green, gradually turning yellow.

Manganese (Mn): A component of chlorophyll.

SYMPTOMS OF DEFICIENCY: Plants exhibit slow growth and yellowing or bleached-looking foliage. Symptoms are similar to those of iron deficiency.

Silica: Builds strong plant tissue.

Homegrown Liquid Feed

Make It

A free and fantastic source of homemade fertilizer is all around you. Believe it or not, many of the plants already growing in your garden are full of quality nutrients and trace minerals that can be made into a tea and fed to other plants. Sounds cannibalistic, but it's already happening in the compost bin—a tea is just faster.

This is a great way to recycle an overabundant harvest. Nothing is wasted. Apply the tea directly to the soil at planting time; spray as a tonic when plants look a little worse for wear or whenever they need a boost.

You Will Need
Gloves

Scissors or shears

A large bundle of fresh herb leaves, stems, and flowers (see sidebar)

A plastic or rust-resistant bucket

1 tablespoon molasses (optional)

1. Wearing gloves, roughly chop or rip all parts of the plant including leaves, stems, and flowers into chunky bits. Toss them into the bucket and add 4 parts water to 1 part fresh herbs. Molasses increases the growth of beneficial microorganisms; add it in if you like and stir vigorously.

2. Set the sloppy mixture aside for 1–3 days, stirring aggressively a few times per day. Regular agitation draws oxygen into the brew to aid in the production of beneficial microorganisms. Beware: If you don't agitate at least once a day, the mix will rot and stink up the neighborhood.

3. Strain out the slurry and toss it into the compost bin or lay it on the garden soil around needy plants. Reserve the liquid in a recycled container or jar and use it as a concentrate. I add a few cups to a large watering can of water regularly throughout the growing season, apply it as a foliar feed using a spray bottle, and pour it on full-strength when transplanting seedlings. Your plants will love it!

Nutrients from Common Herbs

BORAGE: potassium, calcium

CHAMOMILE: calcium

COMFREY: potassium, iron, calcium, trace minerals

DANDELION: potassium, calcium, iron, copper

DILL: potassium, calcium, iron, magnesium

GARLIC: copper, sulfur

HORSETAIL: silica, magnesium, iron, calcium

PARSLEY: iron, potassium, calcium, phosphorous, manganese, copper

PLANTAIN: calcium, sulfur

SHISO: calcium, iron

SORREL: iron

STINGING NETTLE: calcium, phosphorous, potassium, iron, copper

SUNFLOWERS: potassium

TANSY: potassium

WATERCRESS: calcium, iron, manganese

YARROW: copper

TIP: Make a less potent fertilizer using up old, out-of-date herbs from the storage cupboard. Brew it up like a regular drinking tea and leave out the molasses. Allow the brew to cool off before using.

Seasonal Maintenance

Spring

Grooming In spring, older perennials start to show little buds, shoots, and leaves. As they grow, you will begin to discern which stems are done for and which are still viable and green. This is the time to cut out old, dead stems, or reshape woody plants like lavender, lemon verbena, sage, and rosemary that have become misshapen and lackluster. These herbs should never be pruned in the winter, but a light, springtime haircut after the chance of frost has passed helps encourage new growth.

DO THIS TO: Lavender, lemon verbena, garden sage, rosemary, thyme, winter savory, anise hyssop, bay.

Spring Revival When the soil has warmed and new growth has begun to emerge, fertilize mature plants, potted or otherwise, so they can start the growing season with the nourishment they need. Sprinkle a handful of compost, vermicompost (worm poo), or sea kelp around the plant and lightly scratch it into the soil. Be careful to keep fertilizers off the crown or they can cause rot.

DO THIS TO: Scented geraniums, oregano, lemon verbena, stevia, lovage, Egyptian walking onion, and other mature perennials.

Summer

Haircut 101 Midsummer, just before or after rambling perennial herbs like mint and oregano have flowered, is the time to give them a rejuvenating haircut so they'll come back strong for the fall. Think of this as back-to-school prep for the garden. Chop the plant down by half, and use the glut of freshly shorn leaves and flowers to make a recipe like Pesto and Pistou (page 202) that calls for a big batch of herbs, or preserve them now (Mint Syrup, page 184, is a great start) for winter's famine.

DO THIS TO: Mint, oregano, marjoram, lemon balm, catnip, arugula.

Deadheading Remove dead flowers or seedheads before they form to discourage the hostile takeover of aggressive plants such as dill and anise hyssop. Deadheading can encourage a second flush of new flowers on plants that often produce only one and ensures that continuous bloomers keep up their momentum.

Do THIS TO: Calendula, dianthus, dill, nasturtium, marigold, purslane, arugula, lavender, borage, anise hyssop, bee balm, lemon balm, pansy, viola, chamomile, rose, tuberous begonia.

Fall

Prewinter Brush Cut Regardless of whether your climate is warm, temperate, or very cold, most perennial herbs prefer to be cut back hard to within a few inches above the soil line just before winter. Cutting plants back in this way encourages new, tender growth to form for a continued harvest and prevents breakage that can be caused by high winter winds.

Do THIS TO: Mint, marjoram, oregano, lemon balm, hyssop, catnip.

Clear the Crown Old, rotting leaves and stems can hold excess water like a sponge and cause rot around the crown of plants such as lovage that grow in a rosette form. Cut back and remove dead plant matter in the fall and pull any additional debris or fallen leaves away from the crown.

Do THIS TO: Lovage, parsley, sorrel, chives.

Year-Round

Pinching Back Lightly prune off the soft growing tips of basil, mint, and other leafy herbs using your fingertips or a pair of scissors. Pruning a young stem encourages it to branch off and form two new stems, and so on and so on. These mini harvests will eventually lead to a plant that is bushy, stocky, and strong with nice full, lush growth.

Every two weeks or so, remove the top of an entire stem just above a node, the joint where the leaves meet the stem, because this is where a new stem will form. Continue this treatment evenly around the plant to shape it as it grows. You can also use this technique to strengthen light-deficient indoor-grown plants that have grown leggy and weak.

Do THIS TO: Basil, mint, oregano, lemon verbena, scented geranium, thyme, rosemary, shiso, tarragon, stevia, chamomile, cilantro, catnip, orache.

CHAPTER 5

Defending the Plot

Fortunately, herbs tend to suffer from fewer pests and plagues in the garden than vegetables. The aromatic, volatile oils that produce the herbs' potent smell and flavor make them attractive to us. But they function as a defense mechanism that is not very appealing to most insects. In fact, the most powerfully aromatic herbs make good companion plants in the vegetable garden, warding away and confusing hungry insects.

Having a few pests in the garden is completely normal and not cause for alarm. You may not even notice their nibbling as long as there are enough birds, predatory wasps, ladybugs, and other beneficial insects around to keep them in check. Healthy gardens rely on a balanced ecosystem of predators and prey. If there's nothing to eat, the good guys will go on their merry way, leaving your plants exposed to the next wave of pests. As the old adage goes, what doesn't kill us makes us stronger. The same holds true for plants. They'll grow more resilient when they've had some exposure to pestilence.

On the other hand, too many pests and plagues can be an indication that something is off. As a general rule, a healthy garden is a strong one that can take a hit from a harem of procreating beetles, exposure to a fungus, or a couple of busybody flea beetles, and still soldier on.

Diseases often linger in the soil but get their foothold when plants aren't strong enough to fight them off. Herbs that are growing in a pot that is too small or over-crowded, goes too dry or too wet for too long, or is undermined by imbalances such as soggy soil, too much fertilizer in general (and especially at the wrong time), too little light, or lack of air circulation around the leaves don't have the defenses to fend off attack.

Not all insects are pests. Many, like this robber fly, are excellent predators that keep pest populations down. Invite them into the garden by growing umbel and composite flowers such as dill, fennel, chervil, and sunflowers.

Pests to Look For

Diligence is key when dealing with any insect pest or disease outbreak organically. The following pests and diseases are the most likely to show up in your herb garden. The sooner you can identify them and act accordingly, the better your chances of beating them.

Aphids

Without a doubt, these soft-bodied creepy-crawlies are in the running for most hated garden pest. Not to be a downer, but if you don't know them yet, you will soon enough. Aphids feed on tender new growth and leave it gnarled and sickly. They spread disease and are born pregnant, which means they never, ever stop! Why hasn't anyone made a horror movie about them yet?

HOW TO DEAL:

- Spray aphids with water to knock them off the plant, then squish them with your fingers.
- Aphids prefer weak plants with soft, sickly growth. Don't be afraid to sacrifice sick plants for the good of the whole garden.
- Nasturtiums are their favorite meal. Plant 'em near the plants you like, then toss 'em once they get infested.
- Invite their enemy, ladybugs, into the garden.
- Use Soapy Spray (page 57) as a last resort.

Flea Beetles

The image of Lilliputian brown-and-black beetles hopping happily around the garden like they're on microscopic pogo sticks sounds delightful. But then comes the part where they fill your favorite leafy plants with holes and wreak havoc on a bed of young seedlings. Not so cute anymore.

HOW TO DEAL:

- Flea beetles prefer life in the sun. So when possible, plant susceptible herbs in the shade of taller plants.
- Attract their enemies including ground beetles and toads by planting nasturtiums, garlic, or onions nearby.

Leaf Miners

Leaf miners are microscopic fly larvae. They may be too small to see, but you'll know them by the silvery, winding trails they leave behind as they eat their way through the inside of lovage and spinach leaves. They are also sometimes found on basil, mint, lettuce, lamb's quarters, and orache.

HOW TO DEAL:
- Pick off infected leaves immediately to prevent the larvae from becoming adults and spawning a second or third generation.

Scale

Scale insects show up on citrus and bay trees as oval bumps. Often camouflaged brown, they're a hard-to-spot, silent, almost motionless nuisance, and they are nearly impossible to get rid of.

HOW TO DEAL:
- Greenhouses are very susceptible to scale outbreaks. Check all sides of leaves and stems thoroughly in the store before purchasing.
- Attract their enemies, including parasitic wasps and ladybugs, to the garden.
- Remove them by wiping them off with your fingers or using a strong spray of water.

Slugs and Snails

Slugs and snails are eating machines that can take down a leafy plant overnight. There's not much difference between the two. Snails are really just cuter versions of slugs, but they do an equal amount of damage in the garden. Both are found in moist, shady spots. Their numbers wax and wane depending on the year and the amount of rainfall.

HOW TO DEAL:
- Pick 'em and squish 'em underfoot.
- Straw mulch makes a cozy bed for snails, but it also attracts a voracious predator: ground beetles. Lay down wood boards, old pots, or cabbage leaves and destroy the slugs that amass underneath.
- Not unlike frat boys, slugs can't resist beer. To make a trap, fill a cup

or container to the halfway mark with beer and bury it so that it is level with the soil line.

- Scatter crunched-up eggshells or used coffee grounds (applied in moderation) around young seedlings.
- Wrap copper tape around raised beds.
- Raise a flock of ducks(!); they love slugs.

Spider Mites

You're most likely to find tiny red spider mites living on your herbs indoors, especially during dry winters. They show up as lightly colored speckles on the leaves, but you will sometimes find thin webs, too.

HOW TO DEAL:

- Spider mites prefer dry air. Create humidity with pebble trays set underneath plants, mist the air daily with a spray bottle, or install a humidifier.
- Hose down infected plants in the shower.
- Spray with Soapy Spray (page 57) as a last resort.

Whiteflies

Whiteflies are just that: tiny, white, mothlike flying insects. They're primarily an indoor and greenhouse pest that congregates in swarms on the underside of leaves, but they can spread outside, too, if left untreated.

HOW TO DEAL:

- Check the underside of greenhouse-grown plants before bringing them home.
- Repeatedly wash infected plants with a kitchen sink hose or a spray bottle set on stream.
- Sink yellow sticky traps into the soil; whiteflies are attracted to the color.
- Attract parasitic flies and wasps to the garden (pages 50 and 58).
- Spray with Soapy Spray (page 57) as a last resort.

Pest-Free Indoors

It's not easy to keep indoor plants disease- and pest-free for long—it's an artificial environment that can never quite measure up to the outside.

To help minimize problems:

- Check newly purchased or outdoor plants thoroughly for pests and disease before inviting them indoors.
- Use strong lights and replace old or drained bulbs.
- Promote good airflow and humidity.
- Using good-quality well-draining potting soil.
- Keep on top of the watering schedule (page 80).
- Toss out sick plants that have become overwhelmed by pests or disease. They help increase pest populations.

Diseases to Look For

Powdery Mildew

Herbs that become infected with mildew look like they have been dusted with talcum powder. Garden sage, bee balm, calendula, catnip, and roses are likely targets for this fungal disease, so it is especially important to keep on top of the signs and employ prevention strategies, especially as the humidity levels increase around midsummer.

HOW TO DEAL:
- Avoid crowding plants. Mildew is most often caused by high humidity and a lack of airflow around the leaves. Pruning lush growth when the humidity rises can help.
- Always water susceptible plants from below and avoid using sprinklers.
- Chop off any parts that become infected and remove entire plants that are overrun with it.

Root Rot

Plants that droop and wilt, even after a thorough watering, are most likely suffering from root rot. A fungus in the soil is the cause of the problem; however, the real culprit—the root of the problem, so to speak—is poor soil drainage.

HOW TO DEAL:
- Dig up and toss infected plants.
- Improve soil drainage (see page 19). Always add holes to the bottom of pots, and use good-quality potting soil with lots of added grit (page 23).

Rust

Rust is a common scourge of mint and lemon balm that shows up as brown pits on the undersides of leaves and stems.

HOW TO DEAL:
- Remove and toss any infected parts immediately to prevent spread.
- Dig out hopeless cases entirely.

Eating Pest-Riddled Herbs

Leaves that are filled with holes and bite marks left by flea beetles are okay to eat; there's just less left of them. Wash them clean first. Some diseased plants are technically safe, but they taste terrible. I wouldn't go to the trouble of saving diseased plant parts for future use, but eating the best leaves of the bunch won't kill your dinner guests.

Fending Off an Attack

Keeping your herbs healthy and attending to their needs is the best pest control there is. Sprays and powders can be magic pills of sorts, but they come with a price. Using them to eliminate one problem can cause another. First of all, sprays that kill or repel pests have the same effect on the beneficial insects that you need in the garden to pollinate your plants and to prey on aphids, caterpillars, and other munching menaces. Creating a sterile environment where no insects thrive messes up the balance of things and makes weaker plants. Some herbs are sensitive to even the organic sprays. Sure, the aphids are gone, but now you've got a potentially sicker plant on your hands.

Insect Warfare
Spray with Water

Believe it or not, water is the best and safest spray you can employ under attack from soft-bodied insects such as aphids, spider mites, and whiteflies. Sometimes merely knocking aphids off the plant is enough to send them packing for good. Spray underneath leaves, inside crevices, and all over infected plants gently with a hose. If you don't have a hose, a spray bottle set on the tightest stream works. So does the kitchen sink or bathroom shower. Squish the insects with your hands while spraying for good measure.

Finger-to-Finger Combat

Your fingers, hands, and feet are the safest and most effective tools for dealing with an outbreak quickly. It's pretty gruesome, I'll admit, but after an hour spent squishing thousands of teeny caterpillars on a beloved currant plant, I feel oddly satisfied.

Squishing bugs with your fingers is the most environmentally friendly method of controlling an outbreak.

Soapy Spray

Insecticidal soap sprays are effective against aphids, mites, whiteflies, and other pests that don't hop around the garden. However, they work only when the stream comes into direct contact with the insect's body. They will not work as a preventive measure applied to the plant only and can actually kill beneficial insects, too. Use selectively and with caution.

Commercially prepared versions are loaded with fatty acids that dissolve an insect's exoskeleton, causing it to dehydrate and die. You can make your own at home as long as you are careful to use fatty, castile soap brands rather than detergents that are chemical-based.

TO MAKE THE SPRAY:

1. Add 6 tablespoons liquid soap to a 32-ounce spray bottle.
2. Shake thoroughly before each application. Some plants are tender and will be burned by the soap; apply to a small test area and wait a day before spraying an entire plant.
3. Spray the plant, including the undersides of leaves, making sure to target specific pests. If you see burning, dilute the concentration, and always wait until an overcast day to spray.

Strewing Herbs

Strewing herbs is an old practice from the Middle Ages that you can put into effect in your garden today. Potent herbs were tossed or strewn across the floor of houses as an aromatic pest preventive. You can do the same by sprinkling handfuls of dried herbs that are known for their pest-repelling and/or fungicidal properties across the garden soil and over freshly seeded pots to confuse pests and prevent some diseases.

This is a great way to use old, out-of-date herbs that are no longer good for eating. Crush the herbs in your hands before tossing to release their aromatic oils. Reapply weekly or biweekly, or whenever the herbs disappear, especially after a heavy rainfall. Consult the chart on page 59, "Herbs That Can Repel Insect Pests," for specific usage.

Herbal fungicides that you can use against mildew and black spot include chamomile, garlic, cinnamon bark, cloves, ginger root (and leaves), lemongrass, oregano, elderberry leaves, and marigold.

From top: Praying mantises and ladybugs have got our backs when it comes to pests. Both beneficial insects hungrily prey on others, including the much-reviled aphid.

Creating Balance

Building a garden that mimics the diversity of plant life and wildlife found in nature is the surest way to keep pest populations in check organically. The next time you take a walk in a field, look closely at the plants around you. It's not uncommon to see a diseased or infested plant next to one that was left completely untouched. Even plants of the same species won't always succumb to attack by the same predators, depending on their fortitude and what's growing next to them.

New gardens or newly organic gardens that previously relied on chemicals are especially susceptible to attack in their first year. When designing your garden, consider some of the following ways to achieve balance over the long term.

Promote Diversity

Growing lots of the same plant or relatives from the same family in a lump increases the risk of an outbreak that could wipe them all out. Growing in diverse groupings (companion planting) can help repel and confuse insect pests (see the chart on page 59), attract beneficial insects to all parts of the garden, and ensure that if one plant goes down because of a disease, the rest of the garden won't go down with it.

Attract Natural Predators

Predacious insects, lizards, toads, snakes, birds, and bats are just some of the natural wildlife that will feed on pests.

- Install bird and bat boxes and feeders.
- Leave behind stacks of wood that ladybugs can hibernate inside.
- Create shelter for toads, lizards, and snakes by piling up rocks or overturning broken pots.
- Set out a dish of water for thirsty critters.
- Mulch the garden bed year-round to attract ground beetles.
- Leave behind a few dead plants and grasses through the winter to provide seed and shelter.
- Allow dill, parsley, and other umbelliferous plants to set flowers that attract beneficial wasps.

Herbs That Can Repel Insect Pests

Using other herbs to repel pests isn't 100 percent effective, but it's worth a try. Plant the following near susceptible plants to ward off their sworn enemies.

Herbs marked with an asterisk (*) are primarily considered medicinal and not safe for culinary use.

APHIDS: basil, catnip, chives, coriander, elderberry (leaves)*, horseradish (strewing herb or tea), mint, rue*, savory, tansy*, wormwood*, yarrow*

BEAN BEETLES: marigold, nasturtium, rosemary, savory

CATERPILLARS: wormwood*

FLEA BEETLES: catnip, nasturtium, rue*, wormwood*

JAPANESE BEETLES: alliums, catnip, rue*

LEAFHOPPERS: alliums

SPIDER MITES: alliums, coriander

SQUASH BUGS: catnip, tansy*

WEEVILS: catnip

WHITEFLY: alliums, eucalyptus*, rue*

From top: Catnip (*Nepeta cataria*) repels some insects and makes a delicious tea to boot—its flowers, on the other hand, attract butterflies; grow alliums such as chives nearby roses and other susceptible plants to repel Japanese beetles and aphids.

Animal Pests

Raccoons, opossums, and other mammals aren't a huge problem in the herb garden; they're generally more interested in making a feast of hard-won tomatoes, cucumbers, other fruit-bearing vegetables, and tender salad greens that are less aromatic and intensely flavored.

On the other hand, deer and rabbits eat just about anything, but they are particularly drawn to the edible flowers we love best, such as roses, pansies, and sunflowers. They're known for staying away from pungent herbs such as sage and rosemary, so one way to deter deer and rabbits is by using these herbs to make a living wall around the garden in lieu of fences and mechanical barriers.

Our feline overlords pose another potential threat to herb gardens. My cat goes absolutely mental for lemongrass and will do literally anything to get her paws on mine. Keeping her from chewing it to bits has become a yearly battle. Many culinary herbs are safe for pets; however there are a few including Cuban oregano, chamomile, marigold, tuberous begonia, alliums, and scented geranium that can be dangerous to cats and dogs if consumed in large quantities. Get to know what's safe and keep out those that aren't if your pet is a known nibbler.

Squirrels seem to do their best damage in the spring when they dig up new soil in search of the nuts and assorted treats they hid away last fall. Then they are back at it again in the fall, digging in the foods that will become next spring's treasure hunt. Though they are not specifically targeting your harvest, their frenzied digging can do irreparable damage to young seedlings, expose freshly sown seeds and bulbs, and harm the roots of sensitive plants.

To keep mammals off plants and newly dug soil:

- Cover the area with a few fresh citrus peels; they hate the smell.
- Lay down a sheet of chicken wire over newly seeded soil.
- Stick lots and lots of chopsticks or small branches into the earth.
- Protect young plants inside transparent 2-liter milk or water bottles, or yogurt containers and milk cartons with the tops and bottoms cut off.

DIY Barriers

The best insurance against nibbling squirrels and other mammals is a barrier. Protect the harvest underneath old bird and pet cages or cover with chicken wire and netting.

Pesky Plants

Lots of herbs started out as weeds, and their habits haven't changed—just our attitude toward them. Dill weed is a prime example. I will never need to buy or save seeds again, because thousands of seedlings pop up in the soil every spring. I'm not suggesting you stop growing weedy herbs. On the contrary! I grow dandelion, purslane, and several other offenders on purpose because they make good eating. What's important is that you know which ones are the most tenacious so you can control their spread.

There are few weeds that I truly despise. Bindweed (*Convolvulus arvensis*) is one. Its coiling stems can reach out and strangle anything, including garlic, and good luck getting it out once its roots are in. Speed is the trick to dealing with the most noxious, offensive weeds. Take it from me. Even rooftop gardens suffer from the scourge of aggressive plants—their seeds drift by on the wind and take root in pots. No garden is immune.

Weeding isn't just a perfectionist's compulsion. Keeping the most aggressive weeds out of the herb garden is necessary for the health and productivity of your plants. Weeds compete for space, nutrition, and light. Annuals that complete their life cycle in a year are easy enough to control, provided that you cut the flowers off before they set seed.

Perennials like bindweed are the real troublemakers. They spread from their roots, which are often deep or wide reaching. You've got to dig the entire thing out attentively— leave the tiniest piece behind and there will be a new one (or several) next year.

Weedy Culinary Herbs

- Angelica
- Anise hyssop
- Arugula
- Bloody dock
- Borage
- Calendula
- Catmint and catnip
- Cilantro
- Dandelion
- Dill
- Fennel
- Hops
- Horseradish
- Hyssop
- Lamb's-quarter
- Lemon balm
- Mint
- Orache
- Oregano
- Purslane
- Red clover
- Shiso
- Stinging nettle
- Wild strawberry

CHAPTER 6

Making More

When you need more plants, new plants, or perhaps your very first plants, you can go to the store and buy them in little 4" pots, but the dollars add up fast. Fortunately, with a little patience and know-how, there are several inexpensive ways to make more.

Seeds cost only pennies a plant when you buy them by the pack, and if you know how to harvest and save them, you may never have to buy more again. Making mature plants into dozens more doesn't cost a thing—all you need is a gardening friend who is willing to give you a piece. I've never met a gardener who wasn't generous, if not downright pushy, about passing a little bit of his or her botanical fortune along.

Starting from Seed

Any herb that makes flowers will eventually yield seeds. But as a general rule, unless you intend to grow a thyme lawn or you just really, really, really love sage, only annuals and biennials are worth growing from seeds. They germinate quickly and grow to a size that is ready for harvest within months, sometimes weeks.

Perennials, on the other hand, can take ages, sometimes even years to grow into mature plants that are ready to harvest. It makes more sense to spend a few extra bucks on a transplant you can start to harvest almost immediately, but if you've got the patience to grow from seeds, be my guest.

Sowing and Germination

The first things to know before growing plants from seeds are where they will grow best and when to start them. The back of a seed packet or Section Two of this book (page 82) will help you with the *when* part.

Where depends on your climate and the life cycle of each plant. Those of us in the frosty north start tender and tropical plants such as basil and marigolds indoors around late winter or early spring in order to get a jump on the growing season. Starting seeds by this method is a bit of a production, but it's also exciting, bringing a little greenery into your life when the world is still frozen and white outside.

Plastic takeaway food containers are the perfect free alternative to costly humidity domes and seed starter kits. Be sure to add holes in the bottom for drainage, and you're good to sow, er... go.

Grow These Herbs from Seed

Herbs marked with an asterisk (*) do not transplant well. Direct-sow when you can.

- Angelica
- Anise
- Anise hyssop
- Arugula
- Basil
- Borage*
- Calendula*
- Caraway
- Catnip
- Chamomile
- Chervil
- Chives
- Coriander
- Cumin
- Dill*
- Fennel
- Mustard greens
- Nasturtium
- Orache
- Pansy and viola
- Purslane
- Savory
- Smallage (wild celery)
- Sorrel
- Sunflower
- Violet

Soak nasturtium, runner bean, or other seeds with a hard shell in water for no more than 24 hours to encourage the shell to crack open. Rub parsley, bay, and coriander seeds along a piece of fine sandpaper to cut into the hard shell slightly.

Choosing and Preparing Pots

Regardless of whether you are sowing into used coffee cups or objects made of wood, plastic, or any variety of materials found in the recycling bin, always—and I can't stress this enough—make lots of holes in the bottom of your container before adding soil and sowing into them. Seedlings are even more vulnerable to rot than mature plants. Proper drainage is an absolute must.

I typically poke three holes into the bottom of a coffee cup using a pencil or pen. Adjust the number of holes according to the size of the pot or tray used.

Prewash used containers with warm, soapy water. Add a splash of hydrogen peroxide to the water to help sterilize the pots.

Seed-Starting Soil

The soil you use to start seeds should drain exceptionally well, yet hold moisture like a sponge. A store-bought soil-less mix marked "specially prepared for seed starting" on the package is your safest bet and worth the slight cost markup. It's light and airy and has been sterilized as a preventive measure against diseases that could harm sensitive seedlings.

How to Start Seeds Indoors

I like to do my seed starting assembly-line style by preparing the pots and filling them with soil ahead of time. That way I can wash and dry my hands before the precision work of sowing tiny seeds. Keep a scrap towel on hand to wipe soiled hands. This is fun, messy work.

1. Prepare each pot ahead of time by poking drainage holes into the bottom.
2. Fill each container with moistened seed-starting soil to within about $1/2$" or so of the top.
3. At most, sow two mid- to large-sized seeds into a typical 4" pot. Sprinkle several small seeds onto the surface of a shallow tray or a recycled lettuce container from the greengrocer's.
4. Sow seeds thinly or deeply in direct proportion to their size. Plant big seeds into a hole and sprinkle superfine seeds evenly along the soil surface like you're seasoning a meal. Consult the seeds packet for detailed instructions.
5. Lightly cover the seeds with a layer of fine grit, perlite, or vermiculite to keep seeds from tossing around or sitting in a puddle when you water.
6. Place the pots on a tray and water the soil well until it is wet right through to the bottom of the pot. Toss any extra water that is left in the tray after a half hour.
7. From the moment you sow your seeds until they germinate, keep the soil cozy, warm, and evenly moist, like a damp sponge that has been squeezed out slightly.
8. As soon as the seeds poke their heads above the soil, set the pot in the sunniest window you've got and turn it daily so that all sides receive light.

How to Start Seeds Outdoors

It's best to direct-sow plants that do not like to be transplanted or that need a bit of cold weather to germinate. Plant the seeds straight into the ground or into large pots that are already outside. Drainage is still key; however, you do not need to buy special soil or affix a grow light. You'll find that the process is a lot easier because you are not fighting low light levels, dry indoor air, and the fake environment indoors.

DIY Lighting

A grow-light set-up is ideal for seed starting if you've got one. Make your own using a fluorescent shop light equipped with one cool white bulb and one warm white bulb. Place your plants within inches of the lights and keep it running for 12–16 hours per day.

Origami Seed Envelope

Make It

You Will Need

Scrap paper sheets, cut into squares (4" min)

Scissors

This method of folding an origami envelope from recycled paper is quick work. The result is a stylishly simple shape that doesn't require any stapling, gluing, or tape, and it is perfect for storing seeds.

Use scrap paper from out-of-date garden catalogs and magazines, old maps, frayed posters, discarded wrapping paper, or wallpaper samples. Thicker paper turns out a sturdier final product.

Store the filled envelopes in a vintage card catalog, recipe box or shoebox, glass jar, or anything that will keep the seeds dry.

1. Fold a paper square in half diagonally to make a triangle.

2. With the triangle pointing up, fold the bottom right corner up until it meets with the left side. Press the seam flat.

3. Repeat with the left corner until it meets the right side.

4. Fold down the top flap and tuck it into the fold of the front piece to secure.

5. To fill the envelope with seeds, simply pull out the top flap and open it up. Pour the seeds in and tuck it back together.

6. Label each packet with the name of the plant and the date collected. If you can't write on the packet, print the labels found online at easy-growing.com onto sticker paper and affix one to the front.

Seed-Saving Tips

Set aside a portion of the seeds that you harvest for growing next year's garden.

- Clean them and lay them on a piece of newsprint or paper towel for a few days until they are thoroughly dry. You do not need to wash seeds that come from a dry seedpod (e.g., coriander, dill, basil).

- Store them in an envelope or glass jar that is marked with the variety name and date.

- Only save seeds that are mature when you pick them. They should be practically falling off the plant.

Starting Your Clone Army

The fact that we can make baby replicas from the bits and pieces of older plants is kind of freaky and miraculous when you think about it. It's also the only way to reproduce some unusual varieties and stay true to form.

Propagate healthy, strong plants, because chances are good that any diseases they may have will eventually pass along to their plant progeny.

Dividing

Dividing the root ball into smaller plants is good for the health of older perennials that have grown cramped and squished into a tight spot. Creating smaller clumps brings back the vitality of lackluster herbs and prevents root rot.

TRY THIS WITH: Perennials such as mint, marjoram, oregano, lemon balm, hyssop, catnip, French tarragon, and clumping herbs including chives and lemongrass.

1. Dig around the root mass in early spring as soon as the soil is thawed, or in the fall once they've stopped actively growing.
2. Gently pull apart or cut through the root ball with a knife to divide it up into smaller sections. Each piece must have roots and shoots to be viable as a new plant. Pull out or cut off any dead or rotted growth.
3. Immediately replant the healthiest new pieces into separate pots or back where you found them. Take this opportunity to add in fresh compost or soil amenders that will revitalize the plant and help its roots get established in a new location. A thorough drink of water or Homegrown Liquid Feed (page 46) will also help.

Rooting Cuttings in Water

Many soft-stemmed plants will grow roots when you place the stems in water. This is an incredibly easy way to double your basil or mint crop in just a few weeks.

TRY THIS WITH: Nasturtiums, basil, oregano, mint, Cuban oregano.

1. Simply follow the directions for rooting in soil, but place the cut end into a cup of water instead.
2. Top up or change the water every few days.

Rooting Cuttings in Soil

Many herbs with woody stems will produce roots quickly and effortlessly by this method. It's practically criminal how easily you can multiply your stock from one small plant.

TRY THIS WITH: Basil, mint, thyme, scented geraniums, rosemary, lavender, lemon balm, catnip, sage, bee balm, bay, myrtle, hops, anise hyssop, tarragon, Cuban oregano, lemon verbena, savory, stevia.

1. Snip a 4–6" stem on an angle just below the spot where the leaves are attached.
2. Remove all flowers and buds and pluck off a few sets of leaves until 1–2 inches of bare stem remain at the bottom. Set aside scented geraniums overnight to let the cuts scab over slightly.
3. Push the cut end of the stem into a plastic pot or tray filled with well-draining soil, coir, or a mix of 1 part vermiculite and 1 part perlite.
4. Keep the soil evenly moist for 2 weeks to a month, or until the cuttings have formed a healthy root system.

NOTE: This method will not work with parsley, dill, and other umbelliferous herbs.

Grow a Ginger Plant Anywhere

Grow It

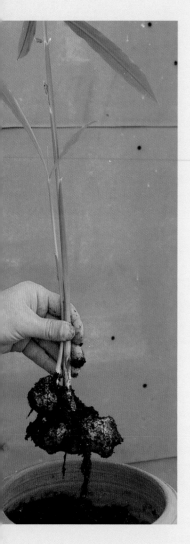

Ginger (*Zingiber officinale*) is a large, tropical plant that depends on a long, warm and humid growing season to develop thick roots (aka rhizomes). If you live in Florida or somewhere with a similar climate, you've got it made—stick a clump in the ground and you're off. As for the rest of us, growing our own fresh crop is slightly more arduous but very doable, even in a pot.

Good Growing

Ginger roots may look small in the store, but with the right growing conditions, plants can reach 3 feet or taller, with single leaves coming in at almost a foot long. Whether in the ground or in a pot, a successful crop begins with gorgeous, fertile soil that can support vigorous growth.

Ginger plants bask in moisture with lots of humidity around the leaves; however, the roots will rot if they stagnate in sodden soil that does not drain well. For this reason, make sure your pot has lots of drainage holes in the bottom and use good-quality soil made especially for container gardening. In the ground, add sand, grit, and lots of compost to help lighten dense or claylike soil.

In the tropics, ginger family plants are grown under taller trees, where they are sheltered from intense sun and gain the added benefit of nutritious fallen leaf litter. Keep your ginger plant in a warm spot that is sunny but protected from direct light. Mulch in-ground plants with straw to keep the soil moist and thwart the growth of weeds. Water regularly and mist the leaves daily to boost humidity in arid conditions.

Planting

Like garlic, potatoes, and a few other root crops, new ginger plants are started using pieces of the root rather than seeds. You can get some cheaply from most grocery stores, but quality can be low because of conditions during travel, and some are treated with chemicals to inhibit sprouting. Organic food markets are your best bet (other than ordering online) because they probably won't have been treated. Look for rhizomes that are healthy and plump, not shriveled, with little buds already forming.

In warm climates, plant directly outdoors in the spring after all danger of frost has passed (if there is any). In cold climates, the best time to start is in late winter so you can get a big jump on the growing season, although I start mine whenever I happen upon good rhizomes, regardless of the season.

Choosing Containers

Plastic tote boxes with lots of drainage holes drilled into the bottom, planter boxes lined with plastic, or food-grade foam produce and seafood coolers are good options as long as they are at least a foot deep. You can grow a plant in a smaller pot, but your harvest will be meager and mostly leaves, not roots.

1. To induce rhizomes without buds to sprout, set broken-up chunks in a shallow tray of light, moist, seed-starting soil and top up with an inch or so of soil. Place the tray in a warm, bright spot and keep the soil consistently moist for several weeks until sprouts appear. A clear plastic bag placed around the tray can help maintain soil humidity as long as you air it out now and again to prevent mold from forming.

2. Transfer the sprouted rhizomes to an in-ground garden, raised bed, or very large pot and space them about 5–6" apart.

TIP: Chopped ginger root and leaves along with a dollop of honey and a slice of lemon make a deliciously warming winter tea.

TIP: Ginger leaves have an invigorating scent and flavor that is a lot like the rhizome, but milder and green. Freshly dug roots are tender, pale, delicate, and incomparable to those mummified things that lose their vigor on the hard-traveled road to the produce bin.

Harvesting

Clip fresh leaves and stems whenever you like. In cold climates, dig the plants up, rhizomes and all, or bring pots indoors before nighttime temperatures dip below 50°F. In the tropics, keep your plants going indefinitely and dig up the rhizomes once the leaves turn yellow and begin to die off.

Grow Lemongrass from a Grocery Store Stalk

Grow It

Lemongrass (*Cymbopogon citratus*) is a lemony, tropical herb that is commonly used to flavor Southeast Asian soups, sauces, and seafood dishes. I like it best brewed with a few slices of ginger root as a hot or cold tea.

Good Growing

Although the plant sounds terribly exotic and difficult, it is really just a grass (albeit a very big one) and much easier to grow than a lawn. This very adaptable plant can be kept small on your windowsill or grown in massive 3-foot-tall clumps outdoors in oversized pots.

Because it is a tropical plant, lemongrass requires a long, warm growing season to reach its mature size. Southern gardeners can supersize their plant and grow it indefinitely in the moist soil near a backyard bog or pond as long as the temperatures never get below 50°F. The rest of us have the option of growing it in the ground temporarily, or planting it in a pot and then shifting it between the outdoors and a bright, sunny windowsill inside.

Planting

1. Begin with a few stalks of lemongrass purchased from the grocery store. Choose the freshest, plumpest stalks that have a bulbous base. No amount of love will revive dry, dead stalks, so hold out for the best you can find. On rare occasions you may happen upon stalks that show traces of root bulbs forming. Scoop those up!

2. At home, peel away the dead outer leaves and trim a bit off the top. Pop the stalks into a jar, cup, or vase with about an inch or so of room-temperature water in the bottom. Set the jar on a sunny windowsill and wait a couple of weeks until roots emerge from the bulbous part of the stalk. Replenish the water every few days so that it stays fresh and the bottom of the stalk is always submerged.

3. Once the roots have grown a few inches long, the plant is ready to tackle life in a pot of soil. Fill a small, 5–6" pot (with drainage holes in the bottom) with rich, premoistened potting soil and evenly space three or four stalks so that the crown (where the roots meet the plant) is sitting slightly below the soil line. Lemongrass prefers to live in a pot that is just a bit too small for its size. Upgrade it to a larger size as the clump expands.

Harvesting

Cut fresh leaves whenever you like. In cold climates, dig up mature stalks in the fall for eating and repot a few to overwinter indoors. In warm climates, cut the plants back to within a few inches of the ground in the springtime to bring them back after winter dormancy.

> TIP: In its natural habitat, lemongrass is adapted to very wet summers and dry, warm winters. To mimic this anywhere, locate your plant somewhere that is always warm and bright or move it around as conditions change. Keep the soil damp like a wet sponge through the growing season and decrease watering during the winter.

CHAPTER 7

Future Fresh

Those of us living in the cold north are conditioned to assume that the garden season ends shortly after summer. As soon as a fall chill fills the air, we mentally and physically prepare to shut it all down and hibernate until spring.

Southern gardeners, on the other hand, seem to live on the opposite end of the spectrum. The scorching heat of summer drives gardeners indoors to cool off while the garden fries to a crisp. Though neither can expect to be as productive as a temperate climate gardener through all twelve months of the year, keeping fresh herbs available year-round is possible, and without the expense of specialized equipment and deluxe grow systems.

This chapter presents an honest look at what can be grown indoors on a windowsill and covers simple, effective strategies that can extend the outdoor growing season into months that were previously considered dead times.

Seasonal Extenders
Raise the Bed
Elevating the bed above the soil line is a simple place to begin. Raised beds (pages 19 and 21) warm up earlier in the spring—giving you a head start—and they stay slightly warmer as the season cools down so that you can squeeze an extra week or so from sensitive annuals such as basil and cilantro.

Mulch
In the spring and fall, apply a thick layer of mulch to keep the soil and surface roots warm through nippy nights. An actual blanket made of burlap works, too, but it is heavy when wet, so be sure to cut big holes around plants to keep it from crushing their crowns.

During the hottest days of summer, mulch acts as a protective shield against the sun's rays, slows down evaporation, and keeps the soil moist longer during droughts.

Candidates for mulch include the following, in order of preference:
- Straw
- Buckwheat hulls
- Leaf mold
- Well-rotted bark
- Shredded newspaper
- Cocoa shells

These exceptionally simple cold frames were made by laying salvaged windowpanes directly on top of raised beds. This is a smart way to warm the soil for early season planting. Cold frames with a slightly elevated back (tilted toward the sun) are even more efficient at capturing light and retaining heat.

Cold Frames

Cold frames are essentially bottomless boxes with removable glass or plastic lids. The boxes are set onto soil, sometimes dug in a few inches, and the clear lids let in light and retain heat like mini greenhouses. If you've got the space, a cold frame is a highly effective way to jump-start spring seedlings right in the garden, and a cozy place to grow salad herbs past the frost.

Cold frames can be made from all kinds of materials, including straw bales and metal or wood boxes. Make a sturdy frame from used timber, an old table, a wooden bookshelf, or your college futon. Make the top from salvaged glass windowpanes or a few more pieces of wood with heavy plastic stapled to the top. Attach hinges to allow the top to be easily lowered or propped up to let in air on sunny, hot days. Cold frames are difficult to use in a container garden but will work set on top of a planter box. Community gardeners can also set aside space in their plot for a frame as long as they don't mind trekking out to the garden to open and close the lid.

Floating Row Covers and Shade Cloth

A floating row cover is essentially just a light piece of cloth that is draped over plants to generate warmth or shade. Nowadays, garden shops sell cloth made from state-of-the-art materials that is ultralight with excellent ventilation. When going DIY, look for lightweight material with an open weave such as lace, netting, or your mom's old sheer curtains. Choose white or lightly colored fabrics for heat, and dark fabrics when shade is what you need.

Water Bottle Plant Shelter

Surround tender annual and perennial transplants with plastic or glass bottles that have been filled with water. Secure the heavy bottles together with duct tape to prevent them from toppling over. The water absorbs the sun's heat during the day and releases it to the plants at night.

This system creates a snuggly, miniature microclimate for your plants that is especially useful in the spring when night temperatures can dip suddenly and drastically.

Bottle Cloches

Clear plastic bottles and milk jugs are the cheapest and easiest way to retain heat in a small space. Just cut the bottom off with a knife and you've got a miniature greenhouse that can be set over an individual plant or pot. The bigger the bottle the better, which is why I hoard and stash the largest water jugs when I'm lucky enough to find them. Glass cloches are admittedly a lot nicer to look at than plastic. Make your own from recycled juice jars and wine jugs using a '70s-era bottle-cutting tool kit. Turning over vintage Mason jars also works well, but you'll need to keep an eye on the plants because they can croak inside without ventilation.

Growing Fresh Herbs Indoors

Once it gets too cold or too hot outside, cold- and heat-sensitive herbs can be brought indoors to live alongside your houseplants. Bring cold-sensitive crops indoors before nighttime temperatures dip down below 45°F or before the first frost. Start early if you've got a lot of plants so you're not saddled with a living room full at the very last second.

Don't bother bringing in plants that look sickly, diseased, or pest-infected—indoor life is hard enough on plants, and only the strongest will survive.

To prepare plants to come inside:

- Give leaves and stems a once-over and pick off any obvious pests like snails, slugs, or caterpillars by hand.
- Set pots in a bucket of water with a few added drops of natural dish soap and/or neem oil and soak for a couple of hours to take care of any critters that may be lurking in the soil.
- Another trick is to give the foliage and soil a refreshing shower with a hose, spray bottle, or watering can with a rose (a perforated nozzle) attached to wash off grime and tiny insects.

Recycled water bottle cloches keep tender herbs like basil snuggly warm through fluke spring cold snaps, hailstorms, and chilly nights.

Dig well around your plant's rootball to help reduce the shock created by shifting it from terra firma to life indoors.

Container-grown plants are easy enough to shift inside, but in-ground plants will need to be dug up and potted into fresh container soil. Yes, it is an added hassle, but even the best in-ground soil will get compacted in a pot and rot your plants' roots in no time.

1. Reduce your plants' trauma by digging well around their rootballs.
2. Lightly shake or wash off as much ground soil as you can without disturbing the roots.
3. Transplant the plants into pots that are slightly larger than their remaining root mass and filled with fresh potting soil.

It's okay to clip some roots back a bit if you need to downsize for space. Scented geraniums, tender sages and lavender, and basil are also excellent candidates for cuttings if you want to go even smaller yet and preserve just a piece of the plant for next year's garden. See page 69 for instructions.

Lighting

Regardless of whether they prefer sun or shade outside, all herbs are going to need the best light you can provide within your home. Unless you live close to the equator, winter days are generally much shorter than in summer. The sun also shines differently; sometimes the light is dimmer or hits your windows at a less direct angle, even when they are south-facing.

Not everyone can afford the price tag or space to house a hard-core lighting system, but I've managed to keep a couple of überfussy plants alive with a clamp-on 10″ metal reflector light and a full-spectrum compact fluorescent.

I'd advise against using incandescent bulbs, but if you do, be mindful of where you rig them up—they get dangerously hot!

Choosing Plants

The truth is that some herbs perform better indoors than others, and a few, no matter how hard you try to keep them alive, simply can't hack it. It's not you; it's your home. Outdoors, plants are subjected to temperature fluctuations (warm days and cool nights), rain, wind, and more intense full-spectrum sunlight.

I've rated the following plants by their fussiness indoors so you know what you're in for next winter.

MOST COOPERATIVE

Little-known Cuban oregano (tastes like common oregano) is the one herb anyone can keep alive no matter how bad the growing conditions. Mine once survived a full month of total neglect and has gone on to thrive and spawn more new and healthy offspring than I can give away.

MODERATELY FUSSY

No matter what you do, chili peppers, stevia, and even scented geraniums tend to look scraggly and a bit worse for the wear after months on a windowsill. But if you can keep them going through the winter, they'll experience a new lease on life after a haircut and a month back outside in the spring.

Rosemary seems difficult, but the mistake is ours. We jump to coddle; however, it's actually a pretty cold-tolerant plant and prefers to stay outside a wee bit longer than other tender perennials. Bring it in right after it has had a chance to experience a touch of frost. Other cold-hardy perennials including thyme, marjoram, tarragon, oregano, and garden sage also benefit from this treatment.

TOTAL PRIMA DONNAS

Unfortunately, sweet basil, the one herb we all want most, is the hardest to grow long-term indoors. With some experimentation I've found that basil varieties with textured leaves such as 'Purple Bush' and 'African Blue' live longer and happier than their soft-leaved counterparts. If you must have fresh sweet basil year-round, consider "Short-Term Growing" (page 81). Short-term is also the way to go with other annuals including dill, fennel, cilantro, and cress.

Keeping Prima Donnas Cozy

Stevia and basil are particularly sensitive to chilly, wet soil caused by drafty winter windowsills. To keep them comfortable:

- Line cold sills with a piece of wool, felt, or old towel to keep pots from absorbing cold through the bottom.

- Keep the entire pot toasty warm with a homemade plant sweater or cozy. Cut the sleeves off an old sweater that was accidentally felted in the wash or sew a tube shape from an old towel or moth-eaten blanket. If you can knit or crochet, make a tube from wool or cotton yarn and add some decorative scallops on top for added flair.

Prune back leggy stems caused by lower indoor light levels to help stimulate new healthy growth. Soft and spindly foliage can attract aphids and other pests.

Maintenance

Adjusting to life indoors where light and humidity are lower can be hard on some plants. Leaf drop is normal, especially in the weeks after they've been transitioned from the outdoors. Here are a few easy tricks to make your plants feel at home inside:

- Treat your plants to a good soak underneath the shower now and again using room-temperature water set on a low spray. This trick can work wonders and is especially useful to remedy infestations of aphids, whitefly, or spider mites. See Chapter 5 for further insight into specific pests.
- Moderate how much and how often you water pots depending on the conditions in your home. Plants set on chilly windowsills tend to stay wet much longer than those kept near drying electric baseboard heaters. Most houseplant herbs do not like to sit in cold, wet soil for extended periods of time, and they prefer it when the top inch or so of soil dries out slightly between waterings.
- Cut back on fertilizers or completely stop all together until just before the growing season returns. Fertilizers force plants into a growth spurt that weak winter sunlight cannot support. Plants end up growing elongated, floppy stems with stunted, sad foliage.
- Prune your plants back regularly to encourage lots of new, bushy growth.

Going Dormant

Keeping your plants in an active state of growth is the way to go if you'd like fresh herbs through the off-season. However, in some situations, you may be better off keeping plants alive in a dormant state, and then coaxing them back to active growth when the growing season rolls around again.

Lemon verbena, Mexican oregano, stevia, fruit sages, and other tender perennials that grow into large bushes with woody stems in a warmer climate seem to do best when they are pruned back hard—almost down to stubby stalks—and put to rest for the winter. Set the plants in a cool but not freezing location with windows, such as a cold greenhouse, apartment building hallway, garage, or basement, and water when the soil has dried slightly.

Short-Term Growing

Grow It

Basil, cilantro, dill, chervil, and other annuals generally don't do well indoors over the long haul. Think of their time inside as a truncated version of their life outdoors.

The best strategy is to grow them from seed as a quick crop that stays small and never reaches maturity.

1. Fill a window box, tray, or pot that has drainage holes in the bottom about three-quarters full with premoistened potting soil.

2. Sow the seeds evenly but much more closely than you normally would. The goal here is to grow a fairly densely packed container that resembles a crop of arugula or microgreens.

3. Cover the seeds with a thin, even blanket of moist soil, set the container on a warm and sunny windowsill or under grow lights and keep the soil moist, but not soaking.

4. Your first harvest will begin in about 2 weeks. Think of this step as thinning the crop to create more space for the remaining plants to develop. Remove seedlings evenly from throughout the tray. Cut the stems with a pair of scissors to avoid damaging neighboring seedlings.

5. Continue thinning the crop every few days until you're down to about 1 plant per inch.

6. As the remaining plants develop, pinch back new growth to encourage them to grow leafier. Harvest a few full plants if they get crowded again.

7. You'll know when your crop has had its day when the plants look ragged and worn or if pests start to make an appearance. Toss the lot into the compost bin and start again with fresh soil and seeds.

THE PLANTS

CHAPTER 8

So Many Herbs, So Little Time

Choosing which plants to profile and which to leave out was a difficult, almost painful process. There are just so many incredible herbs out there that I wanted to share with you!

My main criteria in choosing the herbs that made the cut came down to those that are truly indispensable in my kitchen. I reach for all of these herbs again and again and simply cannot imagine a growing season without them. You will also find a few enticing oddities included that may not be available at your local corner shop or garden center.

As gardeners we are truly fortunate to live at a time when we can use the Internet to make far-flung corners of the world more accessible, whether we're buying plant matter from specialized nurseries or connecting with other gardeners near and far who are willing to share seeds, bulbs, and cuttings.

I hope this section of the book gets you as fired up as I am about the incredible diversity of culinary herbs that are out there. Be aware that growing herbs is particularly addictive. Once you start, I guarantee you'll be hooked.

Legend

Grow

Good for pots

Grown from seed

Grown from bulbs

Grown from transplants

Grows well indoors

Full sun

Partial shade

Shade

Drought tolerant

Moderate watering

Wet soil

Eat

✳ Edible flowers

🌿 Leaves

  Seeds

Stems

Roots/bulbs

● Fruit

Container Culture

Use this key as an at-a-glance guide to growing each of the profiled plants in containers.

- **HABIT:** The mature height and spread of each plant.
- **SPACING:** Spacing in pots and in the ground.
- **MINIMUM DEPTH:** The minimum size pot one should grow in.
- **VARIETIES:** Best or suggested varieties for pots. This is relevant only for some plants.
- **MORE TIPS:** Additional container tips worth noting.

Alliums

Onion Family (*Liliaceae*)

Garlic and chives are the flavoring plants of the edible onion family. They are also kitchen staples—I can't think of a single dish that wouldn't benefit from a pinch or two of at least one of them, and slow-roasted garlic is a late-summer highlight that is not to be missed.

Good Growing

Alliums like full sun and nitrogen-rich soil that is kept moderately and consistently moist, not soggy. All alliums grow from bulbs; the soil should drain well to prevent them from rotting, yet stay wet enough to help them plump up. Consistency is the key. The plants don't produce and sometimes die when moisture levels swing too far into either extreme.

Dig lots of compost into the soil at planting time and apply nitrogen-rich fertilizers before flowering. The same treatment goes for container-grown plants. Overcrowding is another cultural no-no. Onion family bulbs need their space, especially garlic. Chives can take a little bit of cramping but will eventually stop thriving if they are not pulled up and divided. Eat the extras or pass them on to friends.

Container Culture

Keep the soil evenly moist and fertilize with fish emulsion or anything nitrogen-based.

Chives and Garlic Chives
- HABIT: 12″ tall | 12″ spread
- SPACING: 6″
- MINIMUM DEPTH: 4–6″
- MORE TIPS: The deeper the pot, the greater their chance of making it through the winter.

Garlic
- HABIT: 18″ tall | 10″ spread
- SPACING: 4″
- MINIMUM DEPTH: 6–16″
- VARIETIES: 'German Extra Hardy', 'Chesnok Red', 'Siberian', 'Persian Star'
- MORE TIPS: Grow green garlic in 6–10″ pots. Use a very large tub to grow mature bulbs.

Clockwise from top: These chives were dug out of the large washbasin they were growing in when space became tight (all parts are edible); garlic chive flowers taste like a sweeter version of their leaves; newly harvested garlic bulbs are even more delectable than new potatoes—roast in the oven and smush onto bread. Yum!

Chives and Garlic Chives

(*Allium schoenoprasum, Allium tuberosum*)

Hardy Perennial

GROW    EAT

There are two types of chives. The best way to understand the difference is to think of them as miniature versions of onion and garlic. Regular chives (aka onion chives) have grassy, tubular leaves and pink pom-pom flowers that appear around midspring. Both have a mild onion flavor, but the flowers are special as they come around only once a year. Chives are the herbal harbingers of spring. Their bright green shoots are always the first to make an appearance.

Garlic chives are just that—a garlic-flavored, late-season cousin. They have flat, grassy leaves and white flowers that bloom in late summer. The leaves tend to come up later than onion chives, but they are just as easy to grow.

Start either type from seed or bulbs in the springtime. Their bulbs can take the cold, so don't be afraid to purchase scraggly, off-season plants on special and plant them in the fall. Let bulbs go dormant at the end of the season. Don't cut the leaves back. Dig a few up before the ground freezes or shift a small pot to a warm and sunny windowsill indoors. This will initiate new growth so that you can enjoy fresh chives all winter long while the ground outside is still frozen.

Use chive leaves and blossoms in frittatas, cold and warm salads, marinades, dips, soft cheese spreads, and anywhere onions are used. Chive Blossom Vinegar (page 178) is a springtime treat.

Garlic

(*Allium sativum*)

Perennial

GROW   EAT

Gardeners grow garlic for its strong and spicy bulbs, but there is so much more to get from the entire plant. As soon as shoots begin to appear in midspring you can harvest a few to add them to soups and salads as you would chives. Don't take too much, though, if you still want bulbs. Pull up the tender and sweet, unformed "green garlic" cloves in early June. They're mellow enough to eat raw or as a substitute for leeks.

In early summer, winter-hardy hardneck varieties (*Allium sativum* var. *ophioscorodon*) produce a curly flower stalk from the center that is a delicacy in its own right. Chop the delicate scapes into pesto (page 202), or sauté the stems and eat them like asparagus. Later, once the bulbs have fully formed, set a bunch aside for long-term storage, and eat a few right away while they are still "wet." You won't find anything like that in a store.

Plant garlic bulbs in the fall, at least five or six weeks before the ground freezes. If you miss the fall season you can always try again in the spring as soon as the ground thaws, although they probably won't form mature bulbs. You can do the same in pots.

Harvesting Garlic Bulbs

Mature bulbs are ready in mid- to late summer when the leafy growth starts to turn yellow and die back. Dig them out gently to avoid bruising the delicate bulbs. See page 194 on how to dry/cure garlic bulbs.

Anise Hyssop

(*Agastache foeniculum*)—Mint Family (*Lamiaceae*)
Perennial

GROW ▮ ⋅⋅⋅ ♣ ☀ ◌   EAT ✳ ▱ ⋎

This tough old prairie native is a dependable, hands-off tea herb that is adaptable to any garden space. I grew a planter box full of it for years and years in a hot and sunny spot on my roof. I have also grown it in a shadier part of my community garden, where the soil is cool and often dries out. The secret to getting it established is consistent moisture in well-draining soil, but after that it is good to go just about anywhere.

Anise hyssop spreads itself by seeds. I find it impossible to cut the developing seed heads back in late summer when the plant is in its full glory, and then I pay for my hesitation in legions of tiny seedlings the following spring. Still, the beautiful bloomer is at its best when it is given the freedom to fill up an area with hundreds of tall lavender-purple spears.

Brew the licorice-mint leaves or flowers, fresh or dried, into tea or lemonade. Infuse them into milk for ice cream (page 166). Substitute anise hyssop blooms for lavender in shortbread cookies (page 164).

Container Culture
Not suited for windowsills or growing indoors.

- **HABIT:** 2 ft tall | 1-ft spread
- **SPACING:** 1 ft
- **MINIMUM DEPTH:** 10"
- **VARIETIES:** 'Golden Jubilee'

TIP: Grow a healthy crop in wooden planters and extra wide pots or plastic toteboxes with good drainage.

Basil

(Ocimum spp.)—Mint Family *(Lamiaceae)*
Annual
GROW 🪴 -💧 🌿 ☀️ 💧   EAT ❋ 🌿 🌱

Of all of the herbs, basil is the plant kitchen gardeners want to grow most. You can crown me the fanatical director in chief of that fan club, and for good reason. The very essence of summer is captured in the aroma of a freshly picked basil leaf. I cannot imagine a summer without a plant or two (or several) to run my hands across, or a bounty of fragrant leaves to tear over a homegrown tomato and fresh mozzarella caprese salad.

At the end of the season, I never seem to have enough of this aromatic herb—and there are so many different varieties! To begin, I suggest growing fruity mimics such as 'Cinnamon', 'Anise', and 'Lemon'—each one is true to its name and quite unlike the basil you had with last night's pasta. 'Blue Spice' produces an unstoppable flourish of intensely sweet and perfumed flowers that bees and pollinators can't get enough of. Varieties including 'Purple Bush' and 'Spicy Bush' taste a lot like regular sweet varieties but concentrated into smaller packages.

Aesthetically, I favor dark and crinkly 'Purple Ruffles' and 'Perpetual Pesto', a tall, columnar plant with variegated white and green leaves. The puckered leaves of 'Mammoth' are each as big as a slice of bread! 'Purple Bush' is a pretty little plant that stays low and cascades over the sides of pots. 'Siam Queen' grows the best richly red, pom-pom flower heads. In truth, all varieties are stunning when grown en masse, and even more so if you allow a few plants to make flowers— they're sweet and edible, too!

Clockwise from top left: 'Dark Opal' and 'Mrs. Burns Lemon' are delicious dried; the end of season bounty plucked from my small community garden plot; grow enough basil for pesto in a large patio pot.

Container Culture

Choose dwarf varieties for small containers and window boxes. Keep soil moderately moist with excellent drainage. African varieties with textured leaves are more tolerant to drought.

Basil (Tall)
- **HABIT:** 2 ft tall | 1- to 2-ft spread
- **SPACING:** 1–2 ft
- **MINIMUM DEPTH:** 12–16"
- **VARIETIES:** 'African Blue', 'Cinnamon', 'Dark Opal', 'Genovese', 'West African'

Basil (Midsized)
- **HABIT:** 10–12" tall | 1-ft spread
- **SPACING:** 6–12"
- **MINIMUM DEPTH:** 10–12"
- **VARIETIES:** 'Purple Ruffles', 'Spice', 'Spicy Globe', 'Siam Queen', 'Lemon', 'Blue Spice'

Basil (Dwarf)
- **HABIT:** 6–12" tall | 6–12" spread
- **SPACING:** 4–6"
- **MINIMUM DEPTH:** 6–8"
- **VARIETIES:** 'Pistou', 'Purple Bush', 'Minette', 'Boxwood'

Good Growing

Anyone with a spot of sun can grow a decent crop of basil. Most varieties will thrive just as well in a 10–16″ pot as they will in the ground, provided that the soil is fertile and well draining.

Keep the soil moderately moist, but allow it to dry out ever so slightly between watering. If there is one thing basil doesn't like, it's sitting in cold, soggy soil. Yet for a sun- and heat-loving plant, it is surprisingly temperamental about light. It took me years to work out that too much midday sun can burn the leaves, especially when it comes to the soft and tender varieties. All but the roughly textured African types are happiest in a slightly sheltered spot and not in full sun as expected. For this reason, tall, vining tomato plants make a perfect partner in the garden as well as on the plate. Their leaves provide a bit of dappled shade, and the basil, in turn, protects the tomato's roots and repels pests.

Speaking of pests, besides slugs and snails, basil doesn't have many. Most problems come down to the weather and growing conditions; pests seem to factor in only when plants are unhealthy. Fungal and viral problems, specifically Fusarium wilt, tend to affect sweet Genovese types and can be avoided by growing hybrid varieties that have been bred for resistance or avoiding susceptible plants altogether. Pull out the entire plant if it continuously looks droopy or turns brown or yellow (or both), and avoid growing basil in that spot again.

Sowing and Planting

The key to starting a basil crop is patience. It's a fickle herb that hails from warm parts of the world and does not adapt well to cold, wet weather. Garden stores are famous for capitalizing on our enthusiasm by putting basil seedlings up for sale a good month or so before they should be planted outside. Don't succumb to temptation! Basil is always the very last plant I put outdoors; I'll plant it only after nighttime temperatures are consistently above 50°F.

Growing Indoors

Sweet basil varieties have a tough time of it on chilly winter windowsills, no matter how sunny. The problem here is warmth; they need it consistently. I've found that varieties with textured leaves such as 'African Blue', 'West African', and 'Purple Bush' are more forgiving than their soft-leaved counterparts. If you simply must have fresh, sweet basil year-round, try growing it as a quick crop (see Short-Term Growing, page 81).

Transplants are an economical way to go if you're planning to grow only a couple of plants, but seeds are also easy enough to pull off. Start seeds indoors, just before the last frost—no earlier. Plants that have been started too early grow slowly and tend to come out weak and disease prone.

To double your crop quickly, take stem cuttings around midsummer and set them in water to root. See page 68 for detailed instructions.

Harvesting and Using

About two weeks after planting outside, begin to pinch off the growing tips to encourage lush, bushy growth (see page 49). Remove flower buds as soon as they show up to keep the plant focused on making leaves. Both the leaves and flowers of these microharvests make for good eating in salads, marinades, and vinegars. Pull the entire plant up before the first frost hits your region and preserve the bounty by drying (pages 192–194) or freezing (page 201).

Sweet basil is at its best in sauces and soups when it is added in near the end of cooking. Purple varieties taste particularly good dried and sprinkled on pizza; use fruity lemon or lime varieties in fish and curry dishes and in desserts ('Cinnamon' Basil Ice Cream, page 167), or steep fresh leaves in water for a hot or cold tea.

Warnings

'African Blue' and 'West African' are rich and pungent like a spice and an herb all rolled into one. They are intense and should be used in moderation.

Bay

(Laurus nobilis)—Laurel Family *(Lauraceae)*

Tender Perennial

GROW 🪴 🌿 ☀ ☼ 💧   EAT 🌿

Bay is a large Mediterranean tree that is grown exclusively for its gorgeously fragrant, leathery leaves. Sure, you can buy a lifetime supply of leaves at the store for 99 cents, but you may as well throw a few pieces of cardboard or communion wafers into that stew for all the good they will do. Believe me, the real thing is worth the hassle.

Good Growing

Bay is not hardy in areas with freezing winters, which means some of us have to grow it indoors most of the year. Left in the ground, a bay tree can grow to be 40–60 feet tall. Fortunately, they are very adaptable to the size of pot you give them and can be maxed out at 2 feet tall in a 12″-deep container. They're also slow-growing if you restrict their roots, making it virtually impossible to raise a monster that takes over the living room overnight.

Bay does best in a sunny spot with well-draining soil. However, it is very amenable to much shadier conditions and actually prefers protection when the heat is glaringly strong. Plants that are grown indoors should never be plopped straight into the sun, but rather slowly adjusted to the bright outdoor light, and only after the last frost has passed. In temperate climates you can grow bay outdoors year-round, but never plant a seedling that is less than a few feet tall out in the cold.

Use the leaves in soups and stews, to flavor poultry and meat, or to punctuate sauces and sweet puddings, or bake them with apples and pears. Fresh bay has a heady perfume that makes it befitting of uses much more wide-ranging than Saturday night chili. Although that's good, too.

Container Culture

The smaller the pot, the smaller the plant. Keep it pruned and well fertilized.

- **HABIT:** 40 ft tall | 12-ft spread
- **SPACING:** 4 ft
- **MINIMUM DEPTH:** 8″ (seedlings); 12″ (mature)
- **VARIETIES:** 'Aurea', 'Willow Leaf'

TIP: Trees grown in 1- to 2-ft-deep pots can be restricted to just a few feet tall.

Bee Balm

(*Monarda didyma*)—Mint Family (*Lamiaceae*)

Hardy Perennial

GROW 🪴 🌱 ☀️ 🌤️ 💧   EAT 🌸 🌿

Both the colorful flowers and the leaves of this hardy plant are unexpectedly pungent and smoky, similar to oregano. This potency lends the herb to savory rather than sweet foods. The petals are commonly brewed up as a tea or tossed into salads. Lemon bergamot (*Monarda citriodora*) is particularly nice in this way. The leaves are more intense and better suited to fish, meats, or other dishes to which you would add oregano.

Good Growing

Bee balm is hardy and easy to grow. Like all mint family plants, it is ambitious, but I can't say I've ever had a difficult time removing it from where it wasn't wanted. I have to admit, however, that powdery mildew is a serious and hard-to-beat problem. For that reason I am on-again, off-again about growing it. The surest way to keep bee balm happy is to grow it in rich soil that does not hold water well. Prune like crazy to create good airflow, and when all else fails, plant a disease-resistant variety such as 'Marshall's Delight'.

Container Culture

Not suited for windowsills or indoor growing.

- **HABIT:** 2–4 ft tall | 1-ft spread
- **SPACING:** 1 ft
- **MINIMUM DEPTH:** 10"

TIP: Grow a large clump in a planter box or very wide pot.

Borage

(Borago officinalis)—Borage *(Boraginaceae)*
Annual
GROW ·: ☀ ◌   EAT ✳ ⬤ ⅄

Borage is a beautiful, statuesque plant with slightly
succulent and bristly blue-gray foliage. Its cobalt blue,
star-shaped flowers point toward the ground as if they
are falling down to earth . . . bees can't get enough of
them so make sure to plant one close to your vegetables.

Good Growing

Hailing from the Mediterranean, borage prefers setting
down roots in impoverished, well-draining soil. Plants
grown in a fertile spot tend to get too tall and eventually
flop over. Mine always require staking with bamboo
poles, which I suppose says good things for the quality
of my soil. Another trick is to grow them next to tall
tomatoes, which they can use for support.

Once you've grown borage, you'll understand its
pernicious nature—and be left every spring wondering
what to do with the millions of seedlings that come
up everywhere. I learned to throw the young, hairless
sprouts into a salad from an adventurous friend, but
I find the hairy, mature leaves unpalatable unless
cooked. Battered and fried, or buttered and sautéed,
borage becomes a wildly delicious treat with a hint of
cucumber. The flowers also have a fresh cucumber
taste and are said to inspire courage.

Sowing and Planting

In the early spring, direct-sow a couple of seeds
right where you want the plant to grow. Transplants
generally don't take well, but they're worth a shot.

Container Culture

Borage grows long taproots, making it
unsuitable for anything but a very deep
container.

- **HABIT:** 1–2½ ft tall | 1-ft spread
- **SPACING:** 12"
- **MINIMUM DEPTH:** 16"+
- **VARIETIES:** 'Alba'

TIP: Use the flowers (candied or not) as a
dessert garnish or float in a Pimm's Cup.
Finely chop very young leaves and add
them to yogurt or cream cheese as a spread
for dainty cucumber sandwiches. Turn
whatever is left into Homegrown Liquid
Feed (page 46).

Calendula (aka Pot Marigold)

(*Calendula officinalis*)—Composite Family (*Asteraceae*)
Annual

GROW 🪴 ⋰ 🌱 ☀️ 💧   EAT 🌸 🌿

This sunny and cheerful edible flower is one of my favorites for bringing much-needed color to underwhelming corners of the vegetable garden. Calendula blooms tirelessly and attracts beneficial insects. Try peachy/pink 'Zeolights' or two-toned 'Triangle Flashback' if the standard orange and yellow types don't float your boat.

Good Growing

Calendula likes a lot of sun. It's another plant that is prone to powdery mildew in wet and dank situations, so be sure to give it some breathing room and allow the soil to dry out a little between waterings. The plant is an aggressive self-seeder; grow it once and your work is done. It can be grown in a container or window box as long as there is ample depth for its roots to stretch into.

Both the sticky young leaves and the petals are edible. They have a warm, pungent taste that is slightly bitter, but tangy and complex. Add the youngest leaves and fresh petals to spring and summer salads. The petals are more useful as a colorful ingredient in egg and rice dishes. The petals dry easily and store in a glass container for ages.

Container Culture

Can be grown in deep window boxes, but are better suited to medium or large pots.

- **Habit:** 2 ft tall | 1 to 2-ft spread
- **Spacing:** 8–10"
- **Minimum Depth:** 8–10"

TIP: Provide good drainage and ample space to avoid Powdery Mildew (page 55).

Daylily

(*Hemerocallis* spp.)—Daylily Family (*Hemerocallidaceae*)

Hardy Perennial

GROW 🪣 🌱 ☀ ☼ 💧 EAT ✺

Common orange daylilies are considered a garden scourge in these parts. Plant them once and you'll have them for life. Nevertheless, they make a really good edible flower, and that should be reason alone to let a few stick around.

Good Growing

To add insult to injury, daylilies are often referred to as "ditch lilies"—a disparaging yet accurate nickname that points to their resilience and their love for wet soil. Still, mine have thrived for well over a decade in the poor, compacted, often-dry soil next to my apartment building. Go figure.

All colors—not just the orange—are good for eating. Pick the buds while they are still closed, and sauté them lightly. They have a crunchy texture like snow peas or green beans and are well suited to Asian stir-fries or paired with wild mushrooms. That's how I prepared my first taste and it's still my favorite way to eat them twenty years later! The individual petals are good the day that the flower opens and no longer. As their name suggests, daylilies don't keep.

Warning

Daylilies have a laxative effect if eaten in large quantities.

Container Culture

Use plastic pots as they retain moisture longer than terra cotta.

- **HABIT:** 3 ft tall | 4-ft spread
- **SPACING:** 1–3 ft
- **MINIMUM DEPTH:** 16"
- **VARIETIES:** Dwarf hybrids including 'Stella d' Oro', 'Purple de Oro', 'Mini Pearl'

TIP: In cold climates, wrap pots in bubble wrap and overwinter in a sheltered spot.

French Tarragon

(Artemisia dracunculus)—Composite Family (*Asteraceae*)

Hardy Perennial

GROW 🪴 🌿 ☀ 💧   EAT 🌿 🌱

Tarragon is a highly regarded herb that works magic on chicken and vegetable dishes. In fact, it has a bit of a bite that numbs the tongue, hence its botanical name, which means "little dragon." Despite its favorable reputation, I'm a late-blooming tarragon fan. It was my brother's enthusiasm that convinced me to come around. He couldn't keep it in the garden. It's easy enough to grow, but he picked it to oblivion!

Good Growing

Tarragon is a sun-loving plant that does not take kindly to wet feet or high humidity. Whether in a pot or in the ground, the soil you grow it in should drain exceptionally well. Let it dry out a bit between watering as it is prone to rust and rot.

Always grow new plants from transplants only. If it comes as a seed, it's not the real thing. Harvest the youngest, softest leaves for eating fresh.

Tarragon with lemon and tarragon with mustard are two classic flavor combinations that can serve as a base for a variety of meals. Chop fresh tarragon into salad dressings or sauces, or infuse the flavor into butter and spread it on grilled corn on the cob (page 183). Instead of drying it, freeze the tougher, older growth for winter usage.

Container Culture

A wonderful pot plant that can be brought indoors.

- **Habit:** 1-3 ft tall | 1-ft spread
- **Spacing:** 10"
- **Minimum Depth:** 10"

TIP: In hot, humid climates, substitute French tarragon with Mexican tarragon (*Tagetes lucida*), a marigold with edible flowers that can pass for the real thing but with a stronger anise kick.

Lavender

(*Lavandula* spp.)—Mint Family (*Lamiaceae*)
Perennial
GROW ▮ ✿ ☀ ◌   EAT ✳

Lavender is a soothing and addictively fragrant herb. If your only contact has been in the form of a soap-on-a-rope holiday gift set from Great-Aunt Jean . . . I beg your pardon, but you are missing out.

I really wish more people would come around to lavender flowers as a culinary herb. Strong and resinous, lavender has more in common with rosemary than mint. Use it in moderation and you'll be surprised to find how much it adds to both sweet and savory foods. Like rosemary, it suits potatoes and robust meat dishes perfectly. It's wonderfully weird in ice cream, hot cocoa, and colorful summer drinks. Lavender Shortbread (page 164) is not to be missed.

Lavender is broken down into two basic groups: the hardy English varieties and the frost-tender French types. English lavender (*Lavandula augustifolia*) is generally better for eating. My favorite is 'Hidcote', a dwarf variety that is very good for container growing. It has deep purple flowers that are sweet and vibrant. 'Munstead' is another deliciously sweet and compact variety with pale flowers.

French lavender has a camphorous, medicinal quality that makes it unpleasant for eating, but it's mighty pretty to look at with its serrated leaves (*Lavandula dentata*), as is 'Kew Red' or Spanish lavender, with its showstopping flowers.

Container Culture

Allow the soil to dry out slightly between watering.

- **Habit:** 1–2 ft tall | 1- to 2-ft spread
- **Spacing:** 8–24"
- **Minimum Depth:** 8"
- **Varieties:** 'Hidcote', 'Blue Cushion', 'Munstead'

TIP: Space plants about 1 ft apart in the ground.

Good Growing

Lavender is a silvery-leaved Mediterranean herb—that should tell you that it needs dry, sandy soil and a place in the sun. I've tried it in shadier spots; it doesn't work out. Wet soil, especially through the winter, is the surest way to kill it. High humidity is another common problem. When the humidity is high, make sure lavender has lots of space and good air circulation around the leaves.

Cut the plant back in the fall so it will not sustain damage from winter winds, but never go into the woody stems.

Sowing and Planting

Grow new plants from transplants, cuttings, or divisions or by layering stems that touch the ground. Put them out in the spring and add lots of sand, grit, or gravel to the planting hole to improve drainage. English lavender can withstand cold spring weather; it's wet feet that kills it.

Lavender Latte or Mocha

You won't believe it until you try it, but lavender blossoms lend an indescribably delicious depth to coffee and hot chocolate. Whether you drink drip, French press, or espresso, add a teaspoon of lavender buds per cup of coffee to the filter basket and brew normally. Add a teaspoon or so of cocoa to make a lavender mocha.

You can also opt for adding a bit of lavender while steaming the milk, or sweeten with Lavender Blossom Sugar (page 200) after brewing.

Lavender pot, clockwise from top right: French lavender, Hidcote, 'Goodwin Creek', Grosso.

Lemon Balm

(*Melissa officinalis*)—Mint Family (*Lamiaceae*)

Hardy Perennial

GROW ▮ ⋅❳ ♧ ☀ ◌◔ EAT ❊ ◗ ⅄

This light, lemony herb makes for the perfect cup of tea or cool summer beverage and soothes sore stomachs. I've tried using it in cookies, soups, and stews, but it always comes out bland or just plain wrong when cooked. Infuse the fresh leaves into salad vinegar or wine, though, and it magically comes alive. Go figure.

Good Growing

Lemon balm prefers sun but tolerates some shade. Like other mint family plants, it grows best in light, fertile soil that drains well. It is prone to rust if the roots are kept waterlogged. Sow the seeds directly in the garden in the early spring if you wish, but I can't imagine you'll need more than one plant. And because one quickly becomes many, you're better off asking your neighbors for a piece—gardeners who grow lemon balm always have plenty to spare. Fortunately, rogue plants aren't difficult to remove.

Variegated 'Aurea' and golden 'All Gold' varieties are hard to come by in North America, as they are propagated by cuttings only. Someone get on that! However, straight-up green varieties such as 'Lime' and 'Lemonella' are widely distributed. Pick the young leaves in the spring, before flowers appear. Cut the plant back soon after it flowers to avoid spreading more seeds. The little white blooms are lemony, too, and bees adore them.

Container Culture

- **HABIT:** 24-30" tall | 18" spread
- **MINIMUM DEPTH:** 8"
- **VARIETIES:** All varieties grow well, including 'Lime' and 'Lemonella', but try 'Aurea' and 'All Gold' for color.

TIP: Toss the young seedlings and new leaves that come up in the spring into salads. The lemon tang also pairs well with tarragon as a substitute for actual citrus.

Lemon Verbena

(Aloysia triphylla)—Vervain Family (*Verbenaceae*)

Tender Perennial

GROW 🪴 🌿 ☀ 💧　EAT ✳ 🌿 🌿

I've said it before and I'll say it again: lemon verbena is the best lemon herb bar none. Its only drawback—if you can call it one—is that it's almost too sweet for savory meals. Use it to flavor sugar, honey, cookies, ice cream, and alcoholic beverages, or enjoy it chopped on fresh fruit. It makes the best herbal tea around and the leaves are so easy to dry, there's no excuse not to save jars of it for friends.

Good Growing

Provided that you can give it lots of sun and shelter and keep the soil reasonably moist, a small lemon verbena transplant will grow quickly into a rambling, woody shrub. It can produce a very reasonable harvest in any climate, but it will survive indefinitely only in places that do not suffer a frost. Everyone else should bring it inside in the fall (page 80) or start anew in the late spring after all danger of frost has passed.

Container Culture

Don't let the soil get too dry in pots or the leaves will start to burn and grow tough.

- **Habit:** 10 ft tall | 8-ft spread
- **Spacing:** 3 ft
- **Minimum Depth:** 10-12"

TIP: Add a bit of grit or sand to potting soil.

Marigold

(Tagetes spp.)—Composite Family *(Asteraceae)*

Tender Annual

GROW 🪣 ·🌱 🌿 ☀ ◌ EAT ✳ 🌿

My disdain for marigolds was unbreakable—or so I thought—until I discovered the diminutive Gem Series varieties *(Tagetes tenuifolia)*. These marigolds are not the puffed-up annuals that are often meticulously arranged to spell out the name of tourist destinations or take the shape of floral clocks. Their lacy foliage and simple, single flowers come in a range of citrus flavors including 'Lemon Gem' and 'Tangerine Gem'.

Adding these flowers to my plate eventually brought me back around to the African and French types I originally despised. Both are edible in small quantities, but I still find their scent repugnant. The lighter colors are less intensely flavored, and using them is more about adding color to the plate than flavor.

I've recently added two more marigolds to my repertoire. 'Lemon Mint' *(Tagetes lemmonii)* is a tall, shrubby, Mexican native that grows wild in Texas and dry Southwestern states. The entire plant gives off an incredibly potent citrus scent. It's more tolerant of heat, poor soil, and drought than the others and it will grow a strong woody stem within just one season!

Mexican tarragon *(Tagetes lucida)* doesn't look or taste like a marigold. It has a strong anise-like flavor that is reminiscent of French tarragon and favors hot, humid climates.

Container Culture

- **HABIT:** 24-30" tall | 18" spread
- **MINIMUM DEPTH:** 8"
- **VARIETIES:** 'Tangerine Gem', 'Lemon Gem', 'Signet'

Good Growing

Marigolds are tender plants that cannot survive winter in the cold. All are best grown from seed as summer annuals. Sow them indoors 2 weeks before the last frost in your area, or directly outdoors in climates that don't dip below 50°F.

Marigolds like a lot of everything: sun, drainage, and nutrition. They prefer the heat but will start to go crispy along their leaf margins if they don't get enough water. Given enough of all three ingredients, they will keep pumping out flowers until they call it quits in the fall. Deadhead spent blooms to keep the plants producing.

Harvesting and Using

Clip off flowers and leaves and use them as you like. Don't eat the leaves of the French and African types. Pluck out the individual petals and eat those only. Toss a few into a summer salad, sprinkle them on top of cupcakes, bake them into cakes and muffins, or mix them into compound butters. Use Mexican tarragon wherever you would normally use French tarragon (page 99).

Warning

Eat marigolds, especially the African and French types, in small quantities.

From top: French marigolds will happily grow just about anywhere, including this repurposed, vintage Tupperware container; Mexican tarragon (*Tagetes lucida*) is a marigold that tastes just like French tarragon.

Mint

(*Mentha spp.*)—Mint Family (*Lamiaceae*)

Hardy Perennial

GROW 🪴 🌱 ☀ 🌓 💧   EAT ❋ 🌿 🌾

Mint is a refreshing, crisp, and bright herb that is most widely known for its use in herbal tea, cocktails, and desserts. In the ground, mint is like a toddler that hasn't learned how to share. It wants the entire garden for itself, and will push and shove its way into every nook and cranny. Still, the pretty blossoms bring bees to the garden and the plant is incredibly versatile and prolific, so perhaps we will let it get its way, just a wee bit.

No doubt you are familiar with spearmint and peppermint, but they are only the tip of the iceberg. You must grow 'Mojito' mint if you are a fan of the Cuban drink. 'Mojito' mint's warm, deep flavor also makes it a good accompaniment to savory dishes. 'Ginger' mint fares well in a confined space and has really attractive, variegated leaves. 'Orange', 'Grapefruit', and 'Lemon' varieties are the best for making tea and flavoring desserts. If you like peppermint but want something a little different, try variegated peppermint, 'Chocolate' peppermint, or 'Black' peppermint. There is a lifetime of interesting mint varieties to explore. Get growing.

Container Culture
Keep container plants out of really hot sun.

- **Habit:** 10–24" tall | indefinite spread
- **Spacing:** 10"
- **Minimum Depth:** 8"
- **Varieties:** 'Ginger', 'Chocolate' peppermint, 'Pineapple'

Good Growing

Mint is really easy to grow—too easy, really. Problems occur when the soil doesn't drain well enough or when it is consistently too dry. Mint likes rich, moist soil and a sunny spot, but it will tolerate poor fertility and a bit of shade. Cut the plant back hard in midsummer and feed with Homegrown Liquid Feed (page 46) to rejuvenate it.

Growing in pots is the only surefire way to curtail the plant's spread. Potted plants prefer a slightly shadier spot, and the soil should never be allowed to dry out. As long as it receives enough water, mint will grow in a small 8″ deep pot. Unfortunately, it will crowd itself out, and that can lead to disease. It's better off in something much larger and will even overwinter outdoors in an ample tub.

Sowing and Planting

Start transplants in the early spring. No special considerations are necessary. You can take cuttings at any size and at any time.

The same goes for harvesting. Clip sprigs as often as you like. Don't let the flowers go to waste. Use them to make ice cream or as a garnish in drinks and sodas, and on chilled summer soups. Throw out those old factory-made tea bags!

From top: Variegated 'Ginger' mint is a pretty variety that grows well in pots; don't let mint flowers go to waste—they're edible too; add finely chopped 'Pineapple' mint leaves to fresh fruit salad and desserts.

Nasturtium

(Tropaeolum majus)—Nasturtium Family *(Tropaeolaceae)*
Annual

GROW 🪴 ⋰ 🌱 ☀ 💧 EAT ✿ ⬮ ⁂

Round and graceful on thin and wiry stems, nasturtiums are like little lily pads floating and bobbing on an imaginary pond. They are by far the most delicious and uniquely flavored of all of the edible flowers. Kids love them! And so do I.

It's not just the flowers that are worth eating. The succulent young leaves lend a peppery zing to salads, cream cheese dip, and pesto. The flowers are spicy, too, but with a shot of sweet nectar that sits in the spur. Steep the flowers and green, underripe seedpods in rice vinegar to use in salads or on smoked salmon as you would capers.

Good Growing

An old gardener's saying, "Be nasty to nasturtiums," holds true. Nasturtiums should never be grown in rich soil or given too much fertilizer, especially nitrogen. Indulging them in this way is a great way to grow the sort of titanic plant that legends are made of, but don't expect any flowers.

If your garden is already well established and fertile, I suggest growing these ramblers, climbers, and creepers in large, wide tubs that won't dry out easily.

Container Culture

Give pots more sun protection than in-ground plants and never let the soil dry out.

- **HABIT:** 8–12" tall | 1- to 10-ft spread
- **SPACING:** 4–8"
- **MINIMUM DEPTH:** 8"
- **VARIETIES:** 'Empress of India', 'Creamsicle', 'Cherries Jubilee'

Choose 'Moonlight' for its soft, buttercream blooms. 'Peach Melba' is an heirloom favorite that has blue-green leaves and two-toned yellow-and-bright-orange flowers. Dwarf varieties and mounding types are best for hanging baskets, window boxes, and shallow pots. No matter how many varieties I grow, I always come back to 'Empress of India', a dwarf variety with dark leaves and flowers. 'Alaska Mix' is another popular variety that stays on the small side. It has variegated white-and-cream leaves, and the flowers arrive in an assortment of colors.

Nasturtiums, or "nasties," as they are sometimes called, have one drawback: they attract aphids in droves. It's a rare and wonderful occurrence when they make it through a season without an infestation. I usually just spray them off with water and cut the plants back if the population gets out of hand.

Sowing and Planting

Direct-sow nasturtium seeds in the garden after all danger of frost has passed. Presoak the pea-sized seeds for no more than 12 hours and press them into the soil about 1″ deep and 4″ apart. Transplants are available if you forget to get seeds into the soil in time.

From top: 'Creamsicle' is a mounding variety that is perfect for pots; nasturtiums reproduce very easily from cuttings set into a glass of water—this is also a good way to keep leaves and flowers for another day's eating.

Oregano and Marjoram

(*Origanum* spp.)—Mint Family (*Lamiaceae*)

Around here we use oregano, and more recently marjoram, in just about everything: soups, butter sauces, tomato dishes, pizza, and fish all benefit from the savory leaves and flowers. They are a mainstay of our culinary repertoire. Always do a smell test before before buying oregano in the store. Inferior, tasteless types are abundant. You can't go wrong with true Greek oregano (*Origanum vulgare* subsp. *hirtum* 'Greek'). This herb is big: spicy, tingly, pungent, and camphorous.

Good Growing

You'll get the best out of oregano and marjoram plants if you grow them in dry, undernourished soil in a plot that is sunny and warm. A rock garden is perfect. I've successfully kept several types of oregano alive in shadier locations but will admit that it can diminish their flavor and make them more susceptible to aphids. On the other hand, colorful and variegated varieties prefer a little shelter from the sun; otherwise their leaves will burn.

Neither plant can withstand high humidity. Tropical gardeners will have much better luck with Cuban oregano (*Plectranthus amboinicus*), an unkillable, succulent, furry plant that is used in Caribbean cooking.

It's easier to manage the good drainage that marjoram and oregano require by growing them in pots. Both are well suited to small and medium-sized containers. They need a little bit more water than plants grown in the ground.

Sowing and Planting

Both marjoram and oregano are better off planted from reliable, store-bought transplants or received as cuttings or divisions from friends.

Container Culture
Excellent, probably even preferable in pots.

Marjoram
- **HABIT:** 1–2 ft tall | 1- to 2-ft spread
- **SPACING:** 8–10"
- **MINIMUM DEPTH:** 6–8"

Oregano
- **HABIT:** 1½–2 ft tall | 2- to 4-ft spread
- **SPACING:** 10"
- **MINIMUM DEPTH:** 6–8"
- **VARIETIES:** Golden Curly, aka 'Aureum Crispum'; Variegated Oregano, aka 'Variegata'

Clockwise from top left: Oregano flowers are a beautiful and tasty treat; grow bright and cheery Golden oregano underneath tomato plants; round and crinkly Golden Curly oregano softens the edge of a pot.

Oregano
(*Origanum vulgare*)

Hardy perennial

GROW  EAT

From what I have gathered, most of the variegated and colorful plants labeled marjoram are actually oregano. For ornamental purposes I really like the bright chartreuse leaves of Golden Curly oregano (*Origanum vulgare* 'Aureum Crispum'), Gold Tipped Oregano (*Origanum vulgare* 'Gold Tip'), and Golden Oregano (*Origanum vulgare* 'Aureum'). They're a nice way to introduce bright color into garden design, even if you don't care for their milder flavor. Cut all oregano plants back around midsummer and again before they go into winter dormancy.

Marjoram
(*Oreganum majorana*)

Tender Perennial

GROW  EAT

Marjoram is a tender perennial that is difficult to keep alive in places where the winter is cold and/or wet. It is most often grown as an annual and replanted anew every spring. Most marjorams are recognized by their rounded, knotty-looking flower buds—oregano doesn't have this feature.

For something different, try Dittany of Crete (*Origanum dictamnus*). This soft and woolly plant has a name that sounds like something from J. K. Rowling's imagination, and indeed it is remarkably out of this world, yet totally edible. It has silvery white leaves and gorgeously ornamental bracts that dangle like little bells. 'Kent Beauty' (*Origanum rotundifolium × scabrum*) boasts the same dangly bits, but unfortunately it is bitter and a poor choice for spaghetti sauce. Neither of these will survive a cold, wet climate or overwinter outdoors, but they're fun to grow as an annual if you can find them.

Oregano Mimics
These unrelated herbs mimic the oregano flavor and can be grown outdoors in warm climates.

MEXICAN OREGANO (*Poliomintha longiflora*)

MEXICAN OREGANO (*Lippia graveolens*)

CUBAN OREGANO (*Plectranthus amboinicus*)

Pinks

(*Dianthus spp.*)—Carnation Family (*Caryophyllaceae*)
Perennial
GROW ▆ ·⦂ ⚘ ☀ ◌   EAT ✳

Pinks are tasty, miniature relatives of the modern floral shop carnation. The best varieties for eating have a sweet clove taste and smell that will completely blow your mind when you try it for the first time. My favorites, *Dianthus hybrida* 'Rainbow Loveliness' and *D. superbus* subsp. *alpestris*, have elegant and very frilly petals that smell wonderfully sweet. Any of the small clove pinks (*D. caryophyllus*) or cottage pinks (*D. plumarius*) are worth growing to infuse into vodka or wine or to use as garnish for cupcakes and salads.

Dianthus are small plants with grasslike blue-green leaves. They grow best in a sunny rock garden where the soil drains very well. Try them in pots, too. Small containers are fine for the short term. Use large tubs if you hope to overwinter them in the cold. Cut them back after the first flush of flowers and you may see a second budding in late summer.

Container Culture
Pinks are shallow-rooted plants that were made for growing in window boxes and pots.

- **HABIT:** 6" tall | 1-ft spread
- **SPACING:** 6–12"
- **MINIMUM DEPTH:** 6"

TIP: Add a bit of grit or sand to potting soil to aid drainage.

Rosemary

(Rosmarinus officinalis)—Mint Family (*Lamiaceae*)

Tender Perennial

GROW 🪴 🌿 ☀ 💧 EAT ❋ 🌿 ⅄

Rosemary is a comfort plant that exudes warmth. Resinous, piney, and invigorating, its needle-like leaves and woody stems hold up to high heat and slow-cooked meals. It is the perfect accompaniment to grilled vegetables, baked potatoes, and homemade bread.

The plant has its origins in the Mediterranean, where it is a coastal bush. This knowledge is key to understanding how to grow it in the garden. Rosemary isn't particularly fussy or delicate, but it is very specific about what it wants. Getting the balance right can be trying. First of all, as for all Mediterranean plants, soil drainage is absolutely critical. Whether growing in the ground or in a pot, always allow the soil to dry out a bit first before watering.

Good Growing

Rosemary thrives in a temperate climate where it can be grown into a beautiful hedge or planted in drifts that cascade over rock ledges and walls. Cold-hardiness ranges from one variety to the next, but as a general rule, you'll have a hard time keeping the plant alive outdoors year-round if the thermometer dips below 15–20°F.

Container Culture

Increase the pot size yearly or biannually as plants grow.

- **HABIT:** 3-5 ft tall | 3- to 5-ft spread
- **MINIMUM DEPTH:** 10-12"
- **VARIETIES:** 'Blue Boy', 'Tuscan Blue'
- **MORE TIPS:** 'Blue Boy' can be grown in a 4-6" pot.

Rosemary (Trailing)

Cascading plants that trail from hanging baskets.

- **HABIT:** 1 ft tall | 4-ft spread
- **MINIMUM DEPTH:** 10"
- **VARIETIES:** 'Prostrate', 'Foxtail', 'Santa Barbara', 'Huntington Carpet', 'Boule'

Grow new plants from transplants or cuttings (page 69), as the seeds are difficult to germinate and new seedlings will take eons to get to a size worth harvesting. On the plus side, this slow-growth habit can work in your favor. It makes the plants very adaptable to a wide range of pot sizes, and they won't outgrow small gardens overnight.

Prostrate or trailing varieties are the best choices for pots. 'Santa Barbara' and 'Huntington Carpet' make interesting and edible hanging basket plants. I'm in love with a really diminutive variety called 'Blue Boy'. I've got one on my kitchen windowsill, and though it is still too small to clip from, it provides beautiful blue flowers for fresh eating all winter long (page 146).

Taller varieties and more mature plants are better suited to deep and sloping "rose" pots that provide excellent drainage. 'Pink Majorca' is a tall plant with pretty pink blooms, and 'Albiflorus' produces white flowers that look like snow. There is even a golden variegated type, 'Aureus', and a silver version, 'Silver Spires', if you're looking for something radically different.

Harvesting and Using

Harvest stems all through the year, but take less through the winter when the plant is not actively growing. Use the flowers fresh in potato salad or cooked with full-flavored meats. The stems have the same rosemary flavor as the leaves but are less intense. Add the leaves or the flowers to cakes, cookies, and ice cream, such as Orange Rosemary and Honey Ice Cream (page 166). The invigorating, pinelike aroma pairs well with oranges and baked fall fruit.

Prostrate varieties like 'Santa Barbara' grow into impressive bonsai-like forms without pruning or any special effort on your part.

Roses

(*Rosa* spp.)—Rose Family (*Rosaceae*)

Hardy Perennial

GROW 🌿 ☀️ 💧 EAT 🌸 🍎

I've come to regret the bias I once had against all roses as fussy, prissy, difficult, and demanding. As it turns out, I was damning the lot for the horticultural sins of a few. Some roses are all of the above, but there are others—more than I ever could have imagined—that are native to the Northern Hemisphere and practically hands-off. With so many choices available—from tough-as-nails old-fashioned varieties and tiny miniatures to roses that climb, ramble low to the ground, and form thick hedges—there is a rose well suited to every garden.

All roses are edible, but not all roses are worth eating. The very best-tasting roses have the most powerfully intoxicating scent. If you're looking for a cooperative plant that is naturally pest- and pestilence-resistant, look no further than *Rosa rugosa*—a popular, decorative parkland shrub for good reason. Gallica roses, also known as the apothecary rose, are very old heirlooms that stay a relatively compact size. Many of the modern roses hybridized by David Austin are highly scented and easy enough to grow; I favor 'Evelyn', which has a soft apricot flower with a divine old-fashioned rose smell. Fragrant miniatures are hard to come by; however, the name 'Scentsational' says it all. 'Sweet Fairy' (right) is an heirloom miniature with delicious fragrance and delicately soft pink blooms.

Container Culture

Grow climbers and shrubby roses in very deep pots.

- **HABIT:** 1–6+ ft tall | 1- to 6-ft spread
- **SPACING:** 1–12 ft
- **MINIMUM DEPTH:** 12″

Companions

Try growing chives or garlic underneath roses—they can help prevent black spot.

TIP: Grow miniatures in a shallow window box; just don't let the soil dry out.

Good Growing

Roses need full sun and moist, rich, well-draining soil. Water more often around planting time, until they get established. Even the tough types are susceptible (to varying degrees) to fungal diseases. You can manage them by watering deeply at the soil level and keeping water off the leaves whenever possible. Herbal fungicides (page 57) will also help prevent black spot. So does milk. Apply either remedy to the leaves as a spray.

Sowing and Planting

Plant bare-root roses as soon as the soil can be worked in early spring. Add a little bit of compost and bonemeal to the hole.

Harvest rosebuds and blooms whenever they form. Some types bloom continuously from late spring to fall; others bloom only once or twice. Don't remove all of the flowers if you want hips. Wait until shortly after the first frost to harvest the firm fruit; it sweetens their flavor. Leave the wrinkled hips behind.

Warning

Most cultivated roses are susceptible to a wide range of pests and diseases and consequently are sprayed heavily. Harvest only from plants you know have been grown organically.

From top: Rugosa roses are tough and prolific bloomers that will invite a wide range of pollinating insects into your garden; grow the highly fragrant 'Rosa Mundi' Gallica rose as a blooming hedge.

Sage

(*Salvia* spp.)—Mint Family (*Lamiaceae*)

As the poster child of autumn herbs, sage is the quintessential ingredient in stuffing and is most often paired with squash. Not surprisingly, it makes a savory/sweet accompaniment to apples, pears, and other fruits of the season. However you cook with it, the sage you grow in your garden will be drier and more intense than the soft stuff you get from the store. Use a light hand.

Good Growing

Sage plants of all types like a sunny spot in the garden and prefer poor, dry soil that drains very well. Keeping their "feet" dry is the secret to overwintering them in climates that are considered slightly out of their zone. Another trick is to plant sage in the shelter of a warm wall. Resist the urge to fertilize at planting time . . . or at any time, for that matter. Culinary sages grown in rich soil lose their pungent, spicy edge.

When the humidity is high, all sages run the risk of coming under attack by powdery mildew (page 55). Improve soil drainage, avoid crowding plants, and prune or pluck out excess branches and leaves at the first sign of trouble. Unfortunately, powdery mildew is sometimes unavoidable in wet and rainy years—you can improve the soil but you can't control the weather!

Sowing and Planting

Start your plants outdoors from transplants or propagate by cuttings or stem layering. Common garden sage can be grown from seed, but it's not worth the effort because it grows into a formidable bush within just a few years.

Container Culture

Garden Sage
- **HABIT:** 1–2 ft tall | 1-ft spread
- **SPACING:** 8"
- **MINIMUM DEPTH:** 8–10"
- **MORE TIPS:** Colorful varieties adapt best to small pots and indoor growing.

Tender Sage
'Fruit' (*Salvia dorisiana*) and autumn sage (*Salvia greggii*) are best for medium-large pots. 'Pineapple' (*Salvia elegans*) requires a tub.
- **HABIT:** 3–4 ft tall | 1- to 2-ft spread
- **SPACING:** 10"
- **MINIMUM DEPTH:** 10"

Garden Sage

(*Salvia officinalis*)

Hardy Perennial

GROW

The most common edible variety, garden sage (*Salvia officinalis*) is also the toughest of the lot. It can take a cold winter, but tends to succumb after four or so years. 'Berggarten' tastes a lot like garden sage but is much prettier, with very broad, oval leaves and a low, densely compact growth habit. 'Purpurascens', 'Tricolor', and 'Golden' are the best choices for containers, as they stay compact and adapt well to cramped quarters. If you're going to grow sage indoors, these are the varieties to try. They're worth a shot, because they often don't survive outdoors after the first hard frost.

Prune garden sage back in early spring and cut into the green growth only—never go into the woody stems. At its worst, hard pruning can kill the plant, or at least prevent it from flowering. The edible, slightly sweet flowers are one of the best reasons for growing your own! Toss a few into a spring salad or chop them up and infuse into vinegar or softened butter.

Tropical Sage

Tender Perennial

GROW ☕ 🌿 ☀ ◌   EAT ❋ ⬭

Tropical or tender sages are primarily grown in the herb garden for their bold edible flowers. The tubular, nectar-filled blooms attract hummingbirds and pollinating insects to the garden and can be used to garnish salads, cold beverages, and desserts. I find the highly aromatic leaves too bitter to eat as they are, but they make a delightfully unusual tea and add fragrance and flavor to a jar of sugar (page 200).

All tropical sages do well in containers as long as you can provide the right size. 'Pineapple' (*Salvia elegans*) is the pickiest of the bunch—an anomaly of the sage world, really. Unlike other sages it can't seem to take the heat or too much drought. My friend's drooped and dragged like a shaggy dog all summer long until he finally got sick of it. Give it a really big tub to grow in with fertile soil. Keep it consistently moist and move it to a sheltered spot out of the sun and away from walls that radiate heat.

I prefer autumn sage (*Salvia greggii*). It's happier in a smaller pot or windowsill and fiercely rugged, with flowers that come in an incredible range of interesting colors from white to peach to radiant red. Its leaves are vibrantly green and sticky sweet. I can't stop collecting it!

Salad Burnet

(*Sanguisorba minor*)—Rose Family (*Rosaceae*)

Hardy Perennial

GROW ▮ ⋰ ❧ ☀ ◌ ◌   EAT ▰

Salad burnet is such a lovely, ornamental plant. The pretty serrated leaves remind me of tiny palm fronds, and the flowers, when they form, are like puffy red pom-poms.

Good Growing

Start salad burnet seeds outdoors in the cool seasons: spring or fall. It has deep roots and doesn't like to be transplanted. It's a full-sun plant that does well in poor, free-draining soil; however, I've had a lot of luck with it in slightly shady spots with good fertility. It can keep for a season in a small 8″ container but will need to be upsized to something roomier if you plan to grow it longer. Salad burnet is a very drought-resistant plant; just don't let it dry out too often or for too long as the leaves tend to grow tough and inedible.

Keep the flowers pruned back to encourage lots of new growth. Only the youngest leaves are worth eating fresh. Their cucumber-like flavor makes this a good candidate for blending into yogurt, fresh cheese, and Herbed Butters (page 182) and as the name suggests, salads are a given. The herb does not retain any flavor or color when cooked, and the mature parts grow too tough to chew.

Container Culture

Will grow in small pots and window boxes over the short term.

- **Habit:** 1 ft tall | 1- to 2-ft spread
- **Spacing:** 8-10"
- **Minimum Depth:** 8-10"

TIP: In cold climates, overwinter in a deep plastic pot.

Savory

(Satureja spp.)—Mint Family (*Lamiaceae*)

Summer and winter savory are nearly interchangeable herbs that prefer very similar growing conditions and taste, well, pretty much alike. They're a nice complement to sauces, pizza, vinegars, and anywhere else that thyme or oregano is used, but their true calling is in beans. Fresh or dried, summer savory makes beans shine.

Good Growing

When it comes to cooking a meal, I prefer to use thyme, but in the garden, savory can't be replaced. Both plants have thin, spiky leaves and an upright growth habit that stays compact and never gets too tall. Summer savory bursts with tiny, pale flowers in midsummer that pollinating insects go nuts for.

Like their Mediterranean peers, both savories need lots of sun and poor(ish), sandy soil. They don't like to dry out too much, especially right after planting, and do best in a sheltered spot. Pinch back new growth regularly to keep them nicely shaped and leafy.

Both plants are excellent candidates for containers because of their compact size. They don't mind being crowded in a little, and they contrast well next to larger-leaved herbs like cilantro or basil. Creeping savory (*Satureja repandra*) is a very low-growing perennial that is stunning cascading over a pot edge. It blooms in dripping clusters of tiny, bright white flowers.

Container Culture
A superior option for wet climates or where soil drainage is poor.

- **HABIT:** 1 ft tall | 8" spread
- **SPACING:** 8–10"
- **MINIMUM DEPTH:** 6-8"
- **VARIETIES:** 'Creeping Savory' (*Satureja repandra*)

Summer Savory
(*Satureja hortensis*)
Annual

GROW 🪴 ⋰ ☀ ☼ 💧 🌢   EAT ✳ 🌿 🌳

Short-lived summer savory is the preferred culinary
herb of this duo. Its flavor is fresher and less harsh
than that of the winter kind. Summer savory leaves
are slightly rounder and grayish in color. Start seeds
whenever you like indoors, or sow them outside,
directly in the garden in late spring. I have to admit
that I never bother with seeds because my local corner
market sells transplants cheaply in cell packs of
four—and that is all I ever need.

Winter Savory
(*Satureja montana*)
Hardy Perennial

GROW 🪴 🌱 ☀ 💧 🌢   EAT ✳ 🌿 🌳

I've been too hard here on winter savory. Though the
two savories are very much alike, this perennial version
brings a unique peppery spiciness to the dried-herb
rack. It lasts a long time outdoors and is nearly always
available for harvesting, sometimes right through the
winter as its name implies. Don't bother with seeds.
Plant transplants after the last frost. In cold regions,
surround plants with a blanket of protective straw
mulch or bring the plants indoors.

Scented Geranium

(*Pelargonium* spp.)—Geranium Family (*Geraniaceae*)
Tender Perennial
GROW 🪴 🌿 ☀ 💧💧 EAT 🌸 🌿

As a culinary herb, scented geraniums are grown primarily for the flowers, although the leaves of rose and lemon varieties are sometimes infused into sugar syrups, honey, cakes, and tea. The flowers are intense when consumed outright, if not a bit too weirdly geranium. My favorite varieties for taste are 'Attar of Roses' and 'Rober's Lemon Rose'. If you're looking for aroma only, you must try 'Mabel Grey'—its lemon-herb scent is second only to lemon verbena (page 103).

Good Growing

Warm-climate gardeners can grow scented geraniums outdoors year-round as long as the temperature stays above 30°F. Keep them in pots everywhere else so you can shift them indoors and out again with little effort. They're easy to keep this way (page 80) and even easier to reproduce from cuttings (page 68). The bigger the pot, the bigger the plant will grow. Those grown in the ground have no limit and need to be pruned to keep their size and shape within reason.

Put potted plants outdoors once all risk of frost has passed. Some varieties are tougher than others, but it's a crapshoot. Their tolerance for sun, heat, and drought seems to be directly related to their form. I find that the trailing, soft-leaved 'Apple' and 'Nutmeg' varieties need protection from intense sunlight and consistently moist soil, while the roughly textured 'Rose' is practically indestructible. The soft-leaved varieties smell heavenly and fare best in smaller pots; however, they're not great eating. Neither are the peppermint varieties, for that matter. Let your palate guide what you put on your plate and grow the rest for looks and fragrance.

Container Culture

Trailing varieties are better suited to smaller pots.

- **HABIT:** 1–3 ft tall | 1- to 3-ft spread
- **SPACING:** 9"
- **MINIMUM DEPTH:** 8"
- **VARIETIES:** 'Attar of Roses', 'Rober's Lemon Rose'

Sorrel

(*Rumex* spp.)—Knotweed Family (*Polygonaceae*)

Hardy Perennial

GROW 🪣 🌱 ○ 💧 EAT 🌿⅄

Sorrel (*Rumex acetosa*) is a lemony herb with an acidic bite. For this reason it is often overlooked and underused. I like it best as the star of an early spring or fall soup, because these are the seasons when it is softest and most delectable. French sorrel (*Rumex scutatus*) and bloody dock (*Rumex sanguineus*) may not share the allusion to acid in their botanical name; still, they are every bit as tart. Grow them if you can find transplants—they're far prettier and more refined in the garden than their common cousin.

Good Growing

The midsummer sun and heat are merciless on all species of sorrel. It's one of the few herbs that really thrive in cool, damp soil where there is some protection from the afternoon sun. Bloody dock will even work in the boggy margins around backyard ponds. Its roots are deep and require an equally deep pot. Common and French sorrels, on the other hand, are much more amenable to smaller containers as long as you take care to keep them moist.

Use sorrel fresh when it's in season or freeze the leaves after blanching. Cook it like spinach, but serve it in small portions—a little bit packs a punch! Add lots of butter!

Container Culture

Grow in rich, well-draining potting soil.

- **HABIT:** 6–36" tall | 2- to 4-ft spread
- **SPACING:** 10–12"
- **MINIMUM DEPTH:** 10"

Sunflower

(Helianthus annuus)—Composite Family *(Asteraceae)*
Annual

GROW 🪣 ⋰ ☀ ◌   EAT ✳ ⚭

Sunflowers are the reigning queens of the edible flower world. Any plant that can grow to the size of a tree within a single growing season deserves our respect. 'Mongolian Giant' and 'Sunzilla' come in at 14–16 feet tall. That's a lot of plant.

As an edible, sunflowers offer a good return for the real estate they demand. Everyone knows about the seeds, but the young flower buds and petals are also good eating. Add the petals to summer salads and cook the immature buds as you would artichokes. It's a tasty way to make use of end-of-season blooms that will never develop seeds.

Good Growing

Naturally, sunflowers need a lot of sun to reach their full potential. They also need very pliable soil and plenty of water to maintain steady growth. Container growing is possible, but larger plants require no less than a garbage bin to grow deep, stabilizing roots. You can also try dwarf varieties such as 'Sunspot', 'Irish Eyes', and 'Junior' in medium-large pots.

Colorful varieties generally don't produce big roasting seeds, but they are incredibly beautiful. Try white 'Vanilla Ice', multicolored 'Ring of Fire', or my forever favorite, deep red 'Cherry Chocolate'.

Container Culture

Grow large sunflowers in extra large pots and repurposed garbage cans.

- **HABIT:** 1–3 ft tall | 1- to 3-ft spread
- **SPACING:** 9"
- **MINIMUM DEPTH:** 12"
- **VARIETIES:** 'Sunspot', 'Junior', 'Irish Eyes'

TIP: Stake tall varieties with bamboo poles.

Thyme

(*Thymus* spp.)—Mint Family (*Lamiaceae*)

Hardy Perennial

GROW 🪴 🌿 ☀ 💧 EAT ✳ 🌿 🌳

Thyme is an herb that anyone can grow in abundance no matter what their circumstances. It's small, compact, and generously forgiving about soil quality, location, and drought. With so many incredible varieties to choose from, there's no reason to limit yourself. The taste and smell is warm, pungent, earthy, and comforting. It's the ultimate accompaniment to a savory bowl of onion soup and an absolute essential in any cook's kitchen.

Good Growing

In the wild, thyme grows among rocks in very free-draining and poor, often sandy soil. It's a tough plant that can survive a very cold winter as long as its feet aren't soggy. To keep it alive, work lots of gravel, sand, or grit into the soil to increase drainage. Even a bit in the bottom of the hole at planting time will make a difference.

If you don't have good drainage in the ground, grow it in pots. It makes a beautiful showpiece cascading over the sides of a container. Varieties that grow into mounds or creep closely to the ground are very adaptable to just about any size container as long as there are lots of holes for water to flow straight out. The same pots will do very well indoors through the winter and rarely seem to come under attack from pests. Clip off any growth that gets too leggy, and shift the pot back outdoors in the early spring.

Container Culture

Thyme needs more water in pots than in the ground.

Thyme (Creeping)
- **HABIT:** 1–3" tall | 2- to 3-ft spread
- **SPACING:** 10"
- **MINIMUM DEPTH:** 4–6"
- **VARIETIES:** 'Caraway' (*Thymus herba-barona*), 'Creeping' (*Thymus serphyllum*), 'Rose Petal'

Thyme (Mounding)
- **HABIT:** 6" tall | 8–12" spread
- **SPACING:** 10"
- **MINIMUM DEPTH:** 6"
- **VARIETIES:** 'Doone Valley', 'Lime', 'Snow White'
- **MORE TIPS:** Prefers to be slightly pot-bound.

Thyme (Tall)
- **HABIT:** 10–12" tall | 18" spread
- **SPACING:** 12"
- **MINIMUM DEPTH:** 6"
- **VARIETIES:** Silver, 'Orange-scented' (*Thymus × citriodorus* 'Fragrantissmus')

Thyme is so much more than the woody, dried-out stems they sell at the store. Next to the common English thyme, deliciously fragrant citrus types (*Thymus × citriodorus*) are most popular and widely available in garden shops. There are several varieties that qualify in this category—they come in shades of green ('Lemon'), gold ('Archer's Gold'), variegated silver ('Silver Lemon Queen'), and variegated gold ('Aureus'). 'Orange Balsam' and 'Orange Spice' are spicy like orange peel, with pointy leaves that make them look like little conifers. The most compelling are the mimics: thyme plants that smell convincingly like lavender, nutmeg, mint, caraway, oregano, and roses. Bring them indoors for the winter when you can—they're less hardy than the others.

Sowing and Planting

Start a thyme collection from transplants or cuttings, but don't bother with seed unless you plan to grow a lawn. They're slow and sometimes tricky to grow, and many of the unusual varieties won't stay true to form by this method anyway.

Harvesting and Using

Harvest fresh sprigs as soon as the plant starts to emerge in the spring, and prune back straight after flowering. Don't neglect to dry some for off-season usage—the flavor holds up well and is the best way to improve on grilled cheese, baked potatoes, oven-roasted onions, and other winter comfort foods.

From top: Lemon-flavored 'Aureus' is both gorgeous to look at and a useful cooking herb; thyme is one of the few drought-tolerant herbs that take very easily and aggressively to a small strawberry pot.

Umbellifers (Moist Soil)

Carrot Family (*Apiaceae*)

Parsley, lovage, and chervil are culinary cousins of the carrot family that have frilly, lacy, and decorative leaves. I was slow to come around to these unique herbs in the kitchen as well as the garden and thought them to be pretty much the same. Now I can't imagine a year without all three.

To best understand their distinctive flavors, you need only look to their size and form in the garden. Chervil is soft and graceful, while lovage is its opposite: thick, heavy, and larger than life. Parsley sits somewhere between the two.

Good Growing

Unlike many of their herbal cousins, all three of these plants like the sun but hate too much direct heat. They're better off in the shadow of taller bushes or plants where they can get protection from the hot midday sun. They also demand rich, well-draining soil with a bit of compost worked in each spring. Don't let the soil dry out, especially when growing in pots. Chervil and parsley can be adapted to smaller pots if you keep the soil consistently moist and don't expect more than a few months' growth out of them. Otherwise, they're all going to need the deepest containers you can provide. Their roots are surprisingly long, not unlike carrots. And lovage and parsley roots are edible like carrots, too!

Clockwise from top left: Keep a pot of chervil near the kitchen for regular picking; lovage is huge—one plant is enough to feed the neighborhood; flat-leaved aka Italian parsley; curly parsley makes a pretty potted plant—be sure to keep the soil from drying out.

Container Culture

Moist-soil umbellifers grow deep taproots, making them a poor choice for containers. Grow indoors as temporary plants and harvest early.

Chervil
- **HABIT:** 10–15″ tall | 1-ft spread
- **SPACING:** 6–12″
- **MINIMUM DEPTH:** 10″
- **MORE TIPS:** Will grow in a smaller pot for a shorter period of time.

Lovage
- **HABIT:** 5–7 ft tall | 2- to 3-ft spread
- **SPACING:** 2 ft
- **MINIMUM DEPTH:** 12″

Parsley
- **HABIT:** 16–24″ tall | 12″ spread
- **SPACING:** 10″
- **MINIMUM DEPTH:** 10″
- **MORE TIPS:** Will survive in a smaller pot if kept moist.

Sowing and Planting

Direct-sow all three in early to midspring if you choose, although I find only chervil is worth the bother. Its life span is short and you'll use it in larger quantities. Lovage self-seeds if you're not careful, and frankly, you'll never need more than one plant, no matter how big your family.

Harvesting and Using

Harvest the fresh leaves and stalks of any of these plants as soon as they've got a few inches of growth above the ground. Always pick the outer, older stalks first, because new growth forms in the middle. Sow seeds from all three on a window ledge indoors to grow as a quick-harvest winter crop (page 81).

Chervil

(*Anthriscus cerefolium*)

Hardy Annual

GROW  EAT

Chervil is best described as a subtle version of parsley with a hint of licorice thrown in to surprise you. The leaves and flowers are delicate, so use them by the handful. Their flavor and constitution won't stand up to drying or cooking—this is the sort of herb that is at its best when eaten raw or tossed in fresh directly before serving a meal.

Unfortunately, chervil is a bit of an enigma in the garden. It likes the same growing conditions as parsley and lovage; it's just hard to predict when chervil will take and when it won't. It self-seeded abundantly in my community garden plot one year and inexplicably disappeared from the same spot in the next. The only suggestion I can offer is to keep trying. It's worth the heartache.

Better When Burned

Charring fresh lovage leaves and chili pepper skins over an open flame or in a dry cast-iron pan enhances and deepens their flavor. I didn't know the true magic of lovage until an elderly Eastern European woman taught me to crinkle the charred leaves into chicken soup. It's incredibly good!

Lovage

(*Levisticum officinale*)

Hardy Perennial

GROW 🌿 ☀️ ☁️ 💧   EAT ✳️ 🫒 🍃 🌱 🌲

Lovage will never give you trouble in the garden. It's one of the first herbs to show up in the spring, it has few pests, and it will never, ever die. Ever. It's slow to grow, but watch out—mine sat in the corner for years. Apparently it was plotting world domination, because the next thing I knew, it was 6 feet high and rising. It's always the quiet ones . . .

Lovage may be prolific, but it needs a cold, dormant season to reach its full potential. In warm climates, grow it like an annual. The herb is at its flavorful best in the springtime when the leaves and stalks are fresh and vibrant, not bitter. Their flavor is assertive, like a potent, aromatic celery . . . but better. It completely transforms chicken soup and stocks and is simply incredible when toasted and charred first.

A little goes a long way—the flavor is powerful, and too much can cause nausea. The same goes for using the seeds. Smash just a few into mashed potatoes and salad dressing or bake into bread. Infuse a small quantity of leaves, seeds, or chopped roots into vodka or liqueur. I guarantee you it will be a surprise hit.

> TIP: Grow smallage (*Apium graveolens*) in the same way you would grow any of these other moist-soil umbellifers. This tougher, wild version of celery is worth growing in warmer climates where celery just won't take.

Parsley

(*Petroselinum crispum*)

Biennial

GROW 🌱 🌿 ☁️ 💧   EAT ✳️ 🫒 🍃 🌱 🌲

Flat-leaf or curly, that is the question. To be honest, I really can't tell the difference when it comes to flavor, but the majority favor the curly because it's prettier in the garden and on the plate. I find it does a wee bit better in smaller spaces because it stays shorter and is less prone to bolting in the heat.

Parsley needs a bigger pot than you think, especially if you want to grow it over the long term. This is all down to its long taproot, which incidentally also happens to be edible. In fact, 'Hamburg' is a German variety that is grown primarily as a root vegetable. However, all parsley roots are edible, albeit a bit small for cooking. They taste nutty, earthy and a bit sweet—sort of like parsnip.

Umbellifers (Sun-Loving)

Carrot Family (*Apiaceae*)

Caraway, cilantro, dill, and fennel are the exquisite, poised beauties of the carrot family. They look fluffy, feathery, and delicate, yet they're tough, dependable, and damn near impossible to get rid of once they've set seed in the soil.

Good Growing

All four of these ferny plants prefer life in the sun in soil that is moderately rich, evenly moist, and very well draining. Dill and fennel seem to do all right in poor, dry wastelands, but their leaves will grow tough, bitter, and unappetizing as a result.

Spread these plants around the garden at a distance from one another or plan to grow only one at a time; otherwise they will cross-pollinate and undermine each other's flavor and seed production. Do plant them near vegetables and herbs from other families that can benefit from the pollinating insects, hoverflies, and parasitic wasps they bring into the garden in droves.

Sowing and Planting

Dill, coriander, and fennel are commonly sold as transplants, but don't waste your money. They don't like their roots disturbed and tend to bolt as a direct result. Instead, sow seeds directly around mid- to late spring (cold climates) and early fall (temperate to warm climates) exactly where you plan to keep them permanently.

Clockwise from top left: Allow some dill to flower in the garden— it attracts beneficial wasps and is essential for making killer dill pickles; don't let dill seed escape or you'll have a dill forest next spring; garnish black bean soup with cilantro flowers.

Container Culture

Dill and fennel will come up anywhere but are very tall plants that grow thin and lanky in an undersized pot.

Caraway
- **Habit:** 2 ft tall | 1-ft spread
- **Spacing:** 6–8" in 1st year; 12" in 2nd
- **Minimum Depth:** 16"

Cilantro/Coriander
- **Habit:** 6–20" tall | 10" spread
- **Spacing:** 4–6"
- **Minimum Depth:** 8"
- **Varieties:** Look for varieties that are slow to bolt.
- **More Tips:** Keep the soil moist and move to a slightly protected spot in the heat.

Dill
- **Habit:** 2–5 ft tall | 1-ft spread
- **Spacing:** 9"
- **Minimum Depth:** 12"
- **Varieties:** 'Fernleaf', 'Bouquet'

Fennel
- **Habit:** 3–7 ft tall | 1-ft spread
- **Spacing:** 9"
- **Minimum Depth:** 10"
- **Varieties:** 'Bronze'

Caraway

(Carum carvi)

Hardy Biennial

GROW ⁖ ☀ ◌   EAT ✳ ∅ ⁂ ⵊ 人

Caraway is an underappreciated aniseed-flavored herb that is rarely grown and almost never sold fresh in stores. It is known primarily for its seeds, which are used to flavor rye bread and cheese, but the leaves, flowers, and roots are edible, too. Dig them up in the second year before the plant goes kaput. Back in the day, caraway was grown to ward off witches, so if you're not into the flavor, I suppose there's that...

Caraway looks a lot like carrot and suffers from the same pest: carrot root fly. The only way to prevent them is by protecting newly sown seedlings underneath row covers. You can also try planting caraway next to repellents such as sage, onions, or rosemary.

Cilantro aka Coriander

(Coriandrum sativum)

Annual

GROW ▯ ⁖ ☀ ◌   EAT ✳ ∅ ⁂ ⵊ

Adding cilantro to the garden is like growing two, possibly three plants in one. First come the bright and earthy young leaves, followed by wispy, more intensely flavored top growth. No doubt you are familiar with that extra something they bring to fresh pico de gallo salsa and Asian curries. I really like them lightly warmed over a steaming pile of baked potatoes with a little butter and salt. Next up are the seeds: nutty with a piquant and slightly citrus undertone. Only gardeners have access to them when they are underripe and green. Pluck them from the plant when they are plump and brightly colored and the shells are still soft. Time the harvest so that you use them up within a few hours of picking—they'll start to turn brown and their shells will harden almost immediately.

When growing cilantro, keep the soil on the moist side—it's prone to bolting while under heat stress. If it takes off, don't forget to eat the flowers and save a few of the dried seeds to plant your next crop.

> TIP: Toasting brings the flavor out of coriander and caraway seeds. Toss them around in a hot pan until lightly browned, then grind before using.

Cilantro Mimics

These unrelated herbs mimic the cilantro flavor.

Vietnamese coriander, aka rau ram (*Polygonum odoratum*)

Mexican coriander, aka culantro (*Eryngium foetidum*)

Dill

(*Anethum graveolens*)

Annual

GROW ⁃⦂ ☀ ◌ ◖   EAT ❋ ⬭ ⁂ ⚘

Dill is a soothing herb that is nice to look at in the garden. I look forward to its towering, parasol-like flower stalks. Like so many umbellifers, they are an overlooked delicacy that bring beauty to a jar of homemade pickles or summer potato salad. There are lots of uses for the seeds. Bake them into bread and crackers, or sprinkle them on steamed carrots. They dry easily and store for a long time, which is a good thing because you're going to have a lot of them. They stay viable for up to ten years—every gardener I have ever known has a mayo jar full of them in the kitchen cupboard and another in the shed.

Dill is a reliable plant that doesn't require much coddling. I can't seem to stop it from coming up all over the garden, and it will even survive for a time in the thin layer of gravel that covers my tarpaper roof. Lanky container plants almost always require staking to prevent them from toppling over in the wind.

Fennel

(*Foeniculum vulgare*)

Perennial

GROW ⁃⦂ ⚘ ☀ ◌ ◖   EAT ❋ ⬭ ⁂ ⚘ ⋏

There are two types of fennel. 'Florence Fennel' is grown for its bulbous stem and is considered more like a vegetable than an herb. Green or common fennel is a wilder, leafier type that does not produce a bulb worth writing home about. No matter; what we're after are those gorgeous licorice-flavored leaves, flowers, and seeds. Of the leafy type, copper-colored 'Bronze' fennel (*Foeniculum vulgare* 'Purpureum') is my favorite and the only variety I bother to grow. It's very decorative and better suited to growing in pots.

Although considered to be a perennial, fennel is grown like an annual in colder climates because it doesn't survive temperatures below 14°F. Direct-sow the seed in the garden after the last frost and start adding excess sprouts and young foliage to fresh salads and sauces right away. The stems get woody and hard over time but are still useful as homegrown shish kabob skewers or a flavorful bed for roasted fish. Soak them in water first.

> TIP: When steaming artichokes, my friend Gwynne adds a few fennel seeds to the pot. Their anise flavor is a good complement to the artichoke's Mediterranean/North African origin.

Violas and Violets

(*Viola* spp.)—Violet Family (*Violaceae*)

Violas, pansies, and violets are some of the first flowers to show up in the spring, certainly the first of the edibles. Many taste like lettuce, but some are heavily scented and sweet. I once ate a pansy that tasted exactly like a stick of old-fashioned bubble gum. True story.

Good Growing

These colorful spring bloomers are cool-season plants, which says a lot about the growing conditions they prefer. They're easy to grow, but they do not like the heat and start to fizzle out as soon as the summer comes on. Get them into the garden very early in the spring, well before the last frost, if you want to take full advantage of their season.

Pansies, violas, and violets prefer rich, moist soil and partial shade; however, pansies and violas are tolerant to a wider range of sunlight, and violets don't mind it when the soil stays wet.

Eating Violets and Violas

Steep the colorful petals in vinegar, make them into a vibrant jelly, or candy them in sugar as garnishes for cakes and desserts. I use the young leaves to fill out homegrown salads and add the petals to bring brightness and cheer on rainy days.

Container Culture

Keep their soil on the moist side and move them farther into the shade as the summer heat comes on.

Pansy and Viola

- **HABIT:** 4–6" tall | 8–12" spread
- **MINIMUM DEPTH:** 6"
- **VARIETIES:** 'Tiger Eyes', 'Antique Shades', 'Frizzle Sizzle Mix'

Violet

- **HABIT:** 6" tall | 1-ft spread
- **MINIMUM DEPTH:** 8"
- **VARIETIES:** 'White Czar', 'Rosea', 'Freckles'

Pansy and Viola

(*Viola cornuta*, V. tricolor,
Viola × wittrockiana)—Violet Family (*Violaceae*)
Perennial/Annual

GROW  EAT

Pansies and violas are technically perennials, but most gardeners grow them as annuals and pull them out in the mid- to late summer when the plants become ragged and forlorn in the heat. If you can keep them going through this downtime, they'll reward you with fresh growth and blooms in the fall.

Some hardier varieties (usually the violas) will even survive underneath snow and ice and make a reappearance in early spring. In temperate climates you can expect a few to keep blooming all winter long. Cut the blooms back to keep the flowers coming.

Sowing and Planting

In cold climates, start seeds indoors 10–12 weeks before the last frost. Elsewhere, direct-sow outdoors in late summer for spring blooms. Violas are also prone to self-seeding.

Violet

(*Viola odorata*)—Violet Family (*Violaceae*)
Hardy Perennial

GROW   EAT

Violets are commonly known for their highly floral, purple flowers, but they also come in variations of white, pink, and splotchy. They're even easier to grown than pansies because they are hardy and come back on their own with almost no effort at all. I grow a patch in the shadier part of my community plot, where few other edibles will survive.

Sowing and Planting

Ask around before buying transplants—there are always gardeners looking to get rid of a piece of their rapidly multiplying patch every spring. Plant divisions out in the early spring or fall.

Herbal Horizons

The culinary herb world is so much larger than the supermarket aisle would have you think. The following are just some of the edible herbs and flowers I was unable to cover in this book. You should try them!

Other Culinary Herbs

ANGELICA (*Angelica archangelica*)

ANISE (*Pimpinella anisum*)

CALAMINT (*Calamintha* spp.) and

LESSER CALAMINT (*Calamintha nepeta*)

CATNIP (*Nepeta cataria*)

CHILI PEPPERS (*Capsicum* spp.)

CUBAN OREGANO (*Plectranthus amboinicus*)

CUMIN (*Cuminum cyminum*)

EPAZOTE (*Chenopodium ambrosioides*)

GOOD KING HENRY (*Chenopodium bonus-henricus*)

HOPS (*Humulus lupulus*)

HORSERADISH (*Armoracia rusticana*)

HYSSOP (*Hyssopus officinalis*)

JUNIPER (*Juniperus communis*)

MEXICAN CORIANDER, aka culantro (*Eryngium foetidum*)

MEXICAN OREGANO (*Lippia graveolens*)

MITSUBA, aka Japanese parsley (*Cryptotaenia japonica*)

MYRTLE (*Myrtus communis*)

ORACHE (*Atriplex hortensis*)

SHISO (*Perilla frutescens*)

SMALLAGE, aka wild celery (*Apium graveolens*)

SOCIETY GARLIC (*Tulbaghia violacea*)

SWEET CICELY (*Myrrhis odorata*)

SWEET WOODRUFF (*Galium odoratum*)

VIETNAMESE CORIANDER (*Polygonum odoratum*)

WATERCRESS (*Nasturtium officinale*)

Other Edible Flowers

APPLE BLOSSOMS (*Malus domestica*)

BROCCOLI (*Brassica oleracea* Italica Group)

CITRUS FLOWERS (*Citrus* spp.)

DANDELION (*Taraxacum officinale*)

ELDERBERRY flowers (*Sambucus* spp.)

FAVA BEAN (*Vicia faba*)

FUCHSIA (*Fuchsia* subsp.)

HOLLYHOCK (*Alcea rosea*)

HONEYSUCKLE (*Lonicera japonica*)

JASMINE (*Jasminum officinale*)

LILAC (*Syringa vulgaris*)

MUSTARD GREENS (*Brassica juncea*)

PEA (*Pisum sativum*)

PRIMROSE (*Primula vulgaris*)

RADISH (*Raphanus sativus*)

REDBUD (*Cercis canadensis*)

RED CLOVER (*Trifolium pratense*)

RUNNER BEAN (*Phaseolus coccineus*)

SAFFLOWER (*Carthamus tinctorius*)

SAFFRON (*Crocus sativus*)

SHUNGIKU (*Chrysanthemum coronarium*)

SQUASH BLOSSOMS (*Cucurbita* spp.)

STRAWBERRIES (*Fragaria* spp.)

KEEPING STOCK: GATHER, PRESERVE, EAT

CHAPTER 9

Gathering

In addition to caring well for your plants, knowing when and how to harvest will help you reap the bounty at its peak and get the most out of your garden. Most herbs offer up valuable flowers, seeds, fruit, and roots that come into their own at differing times. There are even stages in between that are worth catching.

For example, cilantro and fennel seeds have a completely different flavor when they are immature and green than they do once they've reached maturity and dried out. It would be a shame to miss that stage and the unique opportunity you have as a gardener to access them. Sounds confusing, I know. It takes some practice to learn how to harvest each plant appropriately, and you may miss a thing or two in the first year. But by the second or third time around, you won't miss a beat.

Time to Harvest

One of the benefits of growing your own is the access you'll gain to super-fresh, premium quality herbs that are picked when they are at their aromatic, flavorful best. Every herb as well as their individual parts have a peak that is both seasonal and also down to the time of day. The following guidelines will become intuitive through experience and practice.

- The prime time to harvest herbs, especially fresh foliage and flowers, is early in the day when the aromatic, volatile oils are strongest. Begin after the dew has evaporated, but before the plant has begun to bake in the midday sun.
- If, like me, you are not an early riser, hold off until a day when it is overcast but not wet, or wait until the evening after the sun has gone down and the volatile oils have had a chance to make a comeback. Bring a flashlight!
- Excess moisture reduces flavor and encourages mold to form. Snip small quantities on a rainy afternoon for immediate use, but wait until a dry day to harvest large quantities for drying and preserving.
- If the noon hour on a hot and sunny day is really the only time you can harvest, go for it. Slightly "overcooked" herbs are better than none at all.

Pinching back leafy growth and regularly removing flowers before they turn to seed encourages plants to grow bushier, healthier leaves and more flowers.

You can usually get two decently sized harvests from annuals such as cilantro and dill, although if you cut back too hard on the first go, you may lose your chance at flowers and seeds. Pull the entire plant out if you plan to plant something else in its place. Otherwise, cut it off above the soil line and leave the roots intact so that they can break down and nourish the soil through the off-season.

Leaves and Stems

- To encourage and increase healthy leaf growth, remove flower buds as they appear. Producing flowers, fruit, and eventually seeds takes energy away from leaf production and reduces the quality of the herb.
- Track your plants' season in order to harvest and preserve leaves when they're at their peak. Pick cool-season herbs such as chives and cilantro in the springtime. Hardy perennials including mint, oregano, and marjoram are generally at their best by midsummer.
- Most perennials produce two big crops, although plants like sage need a year to get established and then really "give 'er" (as we Canadians like to say), growing big and abundant in the second year and beyond.
- Biennials like parsley only produce leaves in their first year. When you start to see flowers, collect as much as you can because the plant's time is almost up.

Flowers

- Flower crops such as zucchini blooms and violets are a special treat with a limited blooming season—stay on top of their due date to avoid missing out entirely.
- Watch for a smaller, second flush in the early fall from repeat bloomers such as pansy and viola, dianthus, roses, and lavender.
- A few plants, including 'Sacred' basil, calendula, marigold, and mint never seem to stop blooming once they start.

Harvest Chart

Consult this chart to determine approximately when each herb comes into its best season.

Spring

Arugula

Borage (sprouts and leaves)

Calendula (leaves)

Chamomile (leaves)

Chives (leaves and flowers)

Cilantro (leaves and flowers)

Cress

Dianthus (flowers)

Green garlic

Hops (young shoots)

Lemon balm

Mustard (leaves)

Onion (leaves)

Pansy and viola (flowers)

Sorrel

Sweet cicely

Violet (flowers and leaves)

Summer

Amaranth (leaves)

Anise hyssop (leaves)

Arugula (flowers)

Basil

Bee balm

Borage

Chamomile

Chervil

Cilantro (seeds)

Dill

Elderflower

Fennel (leaves)

Garlic scapes

Ginger (leaves)

Hyssop (flowers)

Lavender

Lemongrass (stem)

Lemon verbena

Lovage

Marigold

Mint

Mustard (flowers)

Nasturtium

Onion

Purslane

Rosemary

Rose petals

Sage (flowers)

Savory

Scented geranium (flowers)

Stevia

Sweet woodruff

Tarragon

Thyme (flowers)

Tuberous begonia

Zucchini blossoms

Late Summer/Fall

Amaranth (seeds)

Anise hyssop (flowers)

Chili peppers

Dill (flowers and seeds)

Fennel (flowers, seeds, and bulbs)

Garlic (bulbs)

Garlic chives (flowers)

Ginger (roots)

Hops (flowers)

Horseradish

Juniper berries

Lovage (seeds)

Nasturtium (seeds)

Parsley (flowers, seeds, and root)

Rose hips

Shiso

Anytime
(Depending on Climate and Availability)

Bay

Citrus (leaves)

Lemongrass (leaves and stems)

Marjoram

Oregano

Parsley

Sage

Salad burnet

Scented geranium (leaves)

Thyme

How to Harvest

When you're ready to harvest, choose the healthiest-looking parts of the plant to keep and use. Discard anything that is diseased or pest-infected. Use sharp, clean tools that can make a tidy cut without ripping or tearing the stems. I prefer to use small hand clippers and scissors on small, leafy plants and flowers. Your fingers are the best tools for pinching back tender, new growth. Shears are only really necessary when the stems are thick and mature. A small hand trowel is handy for digging up roots.

Leaves and Stems

- Always cut sprigs, never individual leaves, or you'll end up with a stripped plant and no new growth. Grassy plants like chives and lemongrass and plants that form a rosette such as sorrel are the exception.
- When cutting from bushy plants such as sage, lemon verbena, or rosemary, avoid cutting into the old, woodier growth. If you cut too far, it can take ages to come back and in some cases won't come back at all.
- Snip from all over the plant to even out the shape and encourage new growth.

Flowers

- Harvest flowers when they are new and their quality is high. Try to catch them just after the buds form, but before they fully open.
- Remove the entire flower, including a piece of the stem. In some cases this will give the plant a chance to produce more. Don't just pluck a few petals.
- When harvesting squash blossoms and other flowers for stuffing, look for blooms that are wide open or just beginning to open. To remove, cut about an inch into the stem with a pair of scissors. Unopened blossoms will open in a vase of cool water and keep that way for a day.

How to Harvest Based on Growth Habit

UMBELLIFERS (dill, fennel, parsley, lovage, chervil): Cut at the base of the stem, or if there are branches (fennel and dill), cut just above a junction where the branch meets the main stem. Cut from the outside of the plant. New growth occurs in the center.

GRASSES (lemongrass, chives) and rosettes (sorrel, dandelion, salad burnet): Remove the entire leaf, cutting about an inch or so above the base of the plant so that it can regrow.

Seeds and Fruit

- Collect immature seeds from coriander, dill, parsley, and fennel seeds when they are still tender, green, and newly formed. Use them up right away, as they will dry and turn brown quickly.
- Harvest mature seeds from dill, fennel, coriander, lovage, and anise when they start to change color and easily fall off the plant. Cut the stems right back; don't bother trying to harvest individual seeds off the plant.
- Hold a box underneath large seed heads as you cut them to avoid losing falling seeds.

Roots and Bulbs

- Roots generally reach their prime at the end of a long growing season, once they've had a chance to mature and develop their flavor in the soil. The top growth of the plant is typically on the way out by this point.
- Wait until the soil has been dry for a few days, especially when digging bulbs like garlic.
- Dig well around the base of the plant to avoid bruising or piercing roots and bulbs. Use a small hand trowel, your hands, or a fork to lift them out of the soil. Tip containers onto a plastic sheet for easy access.
- Shake and wash off the soil from horseradish and other firm roots, but do not wash garlic, onions, and other bulbs you intend to store.
- Cut off the part of the plant that grew above the soil line and trim off root hairs and small side roots.

From top: Separate dried coriander seeds from their stems easily by pinching and pulling forward with your fingers; blow away additional bits and pieces or shake in the wind.

Herbal Bouquet

Make It

A bouquet of culinary herbs and flowers picked fresh from your garden makes an impressive housewarming gift that is so much more personal and practical and better for the environment than a random bouquet of tea roses shipped from Central America. I made one for my brother when he moved into a new apartment and it actually had an impact on his cooking by introducing him to fresh herbs he had never tried before.

Presentation

Assemble the fresh-cut herbs in an aesthetically pleasing way, taking colors and texture into account. Your wrapping job doesn't have to be perfect—in fact, imperfection is charming. Here are a few ideas:

- Wrap lots of butcher twine, colorful string, raffia, or embroidery thread around the stem ends to tie them together.
- Bundle the herbs together and package them up in a pretty piece of paper, just like you'd find in a floral shop. Use a piece of parchment or newsprint with a short length of jute tied around the bottom, or make it colorful using patterned wrapping paper.
- Wrap a piece of cheesecloth or scrap fabric around the bottom first, and secure it in place with another strip of fabric or twine tied into a knot or bow.

Make a little information tag that identifies the herbs and offers suggestions on how to cook with them. Or you can just skip the formality and tell your friend in person.

Keep It Fresh

Some herbs start to wilt immediately in hot weather. To keep them fresh longer, wrap the stem ends in a moistened fabric or paper towel. Slip the wet end into a plastic bag or wrap with plastic wrap or foil to lock in moisture and keep the wetness from soiling your beautifully crafted presentation.

Ideas to Get You Started

Herbes de Provence
Rosemary, thyme, marjoram, lavender, chervil
USES: SOUPS, POULTRY, CASSEROLES

Hierba de Olor
Oregano, bay, marjoram, thyme
USES: MEXICAN SOUPS AND STEWS

Stuffing
Rosemary, bay, sage, thyme, parsley
USES: STUFFING, STEWS, HEARTY SOUPS

Salad Herbs
Calendula, dill, cilantro, basil, purslane, sorrel, parsley, violets, chive blossoms, salad burnet
USES: SEE PAGES 162–163

Medley
A mixture of one type of herb, in different varieties. For example, three different varieties of basil or mint.

Cocktail Hour
'Mojito' Mint, 'Purple' shiso, rosemary, basil, tarragon, lemon balm
USES: MOJITOS, MARTINIS, HERB-INFUSED VODKA (PAGES 186, 190–191)

Herbal Tisanes
Chamomile, peppermint, 'Ginger' mint, bee balm, lemon verbena, lavender, lemon balm
USES: SEE PAGE 195

Thai Cuisine
Chili peppers, lemongrass, mint, 'Sacred' basil, 'Thai' basil
USES: PAD THAI, THAI SHRIMP BASIL, LEMONGRASS CHICKEN, TOM YUM SOUP

CHAPTER 10

Herbs: From the Garden to Your Belly

As you delve further into growing herbs, you'll be naturally enticed to try more exotic varieties and plants that you've never even heard of. There are so many herbs, countless flavors, and nearly limitless, divergent ways to prepare, alter, and subvert them—the possibilities are pretty near endless.

Decades into growing my own edibles, I am still pleasantly surprised, if not humbled, by how much there is to know about the most basic, everyday herbs like parsley, dill, and basil. And yet from time to time I find myself falling into a familiar, albeit delicious routine with these old favorites.

As you develop a relationship with the herbs you grow, don't forget to take a new look at the old standbys now and again. Remove them from the same old context and find inspiration in other countries that use them to different effect. Sprinkle rosemary on something other than potatoes. Put fresh basil into ice cream instead of pasta. Pound, macerate, tear, or grind your favorite herb rather than chopping it. Char its leaves, taste its flowers, batter and fry it, or brew it into tea. Serve big sprigs of fresh herbs by the handful as a salad or an appetizer alongside salty cheese and warm bread where they can be appreciated as they are, as more than just a flavoring.

However you use your herbs, as a grower you've always got a leg up because fresh herbs are at their very best directly after picking. Even the average, everyday herb used in an average, everyday way is going to be a million times better than anything bought in a store.

The pages that follow include some of my favorite seasonal treats that are best made throughout the growing season with freshly picked herbs and flowers from the garden. I've also included a few less-than-usual delicacies that I hope will inspire you to try old flavors in new ways and new flavors in place of everyday staples.

Use these images of mint at various stages of preparation as a guide to chopping up herbs for recipes in this book. Clockwise from top left: one sprig; whole leaves; roughly chopped; chopped.

Washing and Drying Herbs

Wash leafy herbs that you are about to use and cook immediately or freeze, but don't wash foliage that you plan to dry for long-term storage. No matter how good your drying efforts, wetting the leaves makes them dry brown and will only increase your chances of growing mold.

Rinse the caked-on mud from around knobby roots. Scrub gently with a brush to get inside the nooks and crannies. I don't bother with little bits of dirt because it's easy enough to flake or rub off once dried. Don't wash garlic or onion bulbs, because moisture inhibits the curing/drying process.

After washing, dry individual leaves and small sprigs in a salad spinner and pat them between two layers of kitchen towel. In lieu of a salad spinner, or when drying off large stems, pile the herbs into one end of a clean, dry kitchen towel and roll it into a tube. Bring the ends together, twist, and shake vigorously so that the towel can soak up the moisture.

How to Remove Leaves

Sorrel, cilantro, dill, lovage, parsley, 'Bronze' fennel, and chervil have soft stems nearer to the top or outer edges of the plant that are best for using fresh. Hard and woody stems hold flavor, but picking wiry strands of oregano out of your teeth can really sour a meal. To test for tenderness, try to break a stem with your fingers. Anything that puts up a fight needs to be separated from the delectable bits before you add it to your meal.

The fastest way to defoliate a stem of oregano, tarragon, rosemary, or other small-leaved herbs is to strip the leaves off against the grain of their growth. Hold the top end of the stem with the index finger and thumb of one hand and pull down on the leaves with the finger and thumb of the other. The leaves should just slide off. Pinch and pluck large leaves off their stems using your fingers, or chop them off with a knife or a pair of scissors.

Waste Not

The tough, defoliated stems of basil, sage, oregano, savory, lemon balm, and fennel (to name a few) are full of flavor; it's a shame to throw them away. Extract a little extra mileage from your hard work by tossing them into soup stock. Use them to line the bottom of a roasting pan when cooking duck, chicken, or other meats. The stems create a reservoir for drippings and infuse the meat with flavor. This will work with potatoes and vegetables, too, but you may need to add some liquid to keep them from drying out.

Making Smaller Bits

There are about a hundred ways to Sunday to break down fresh leaves, roots, bulbs, seeds, and fruit into smaller pieces.

Tearing: Ripping rough pieces with your fingers is the classic way to prepare basil leaves. Italians say it tastes better this way. I like that there are fewer utensils to wash.

Smashing and pounding: Lightly pound or crush garlic cloves, ginger, lemongrass, dried leaves, hard seeds, and woody stems with a heavy rolling pin, a cast-iron pan, or a mortar and pestle to release their flavor. I like this technique when I want to infuse a meal with an intense flavor such as garlic or bay, and then remove the herb partway through cooking.

Chopping: Always use a sharp knife to avoid bruising the herbs and accidentally removing your own body parts. You don't need anything too fancy; just a pair of scissors or a big knife of decent quality and a flat cutting board. See the photo on page 151 for my interpretation of the varying grades of chopped herb sizes used in this book.

Chiffonade: This French technique is a way to chop basil, sorrel, sage, and other large-leaved herbs into impressive, elegant ribbons. Stack the leaves into small piles, roll them up into a tube, and, using a sharp knife, quickly slice across into thin strips.

Borage Fritters

Ingredients

1 cup flour

¼ teaspoon sea salt, plus more to taste

2 eggs, separated

1 tablespoon olive oil

¾ cup sparkling water, chilled

1½ cups roughly chopped fresh borage leaves

¼ cup grated hard Italian cheese (Parmesan or Pecorino)

Canola oil for frying

Lemon juice (optional)

Crème fraîche or yogurt

Serves 5

These crispy little fritters are a tasty way to make use of a spring borage invasion. The fried leaves have a mild cucumbery taste—cooking removes all trace of their scratchy prickles. Come late summer when the big boys start to look scraggly, I pick off the youngest, greenest growth and make fritters again. The rest goes into the compost heap.

1. In a large bowl, sift the flour with the salt. Add the egg yolks, oil, and sparkling water and whisk until you have a smooth batter.

2. In a medium bowl, whisk the egg whites until soft peaks are formed, and fold them into the batter. Gently stir in the borage leaves and grated cheese.

3. Heat ¼ inch oil in a medium saucepan over medium heat. Slide tablespoons of batter into the hot oil and fry until both sides are crispy and golden brown, about 3 minutes. Turn halfway through when just the portion poking above the oil is raw.

4. Remove from the oil with a slotted spoon and set on a plate or platter lined with paper towels.

5. Sprinkle with salt and a squeeze of lemon juice, and serve warm with a dollop of crème fraîche.

Stuffed Squash Blossoms

Ingredients

½ cup ricotta cheese

2 tablespoons grated Parmesan or Pecorino cheese

1 tablespoon finely chopped fresh basil leaves

1 tablespoon finely chopped fresh chives

1 teaspoon finely chopped fresh oregano leaves

Pinch of sea salt, plus more to taste

Milk (optional)

1 cup sparkling water

1 cup flour

10 zucchini blossoms

Canola oil for frying

Makes 10 flowers (about 5 servings)

Squash blossoms stuffed with cheese and herbs and fried in batter are a summer delicacy I eagerly await from the moment the seeds go into the soil. Unfortunately squash blossoms do not travel or keep well, making this a truly seasonal food that comes around for only a short time once a year. Get it while you can!

You can substitute squash blossoms with Rose of Sharon (*Hibiscus syriacus*) or hollyhocks (*Alcea rosea*), but to be honest, it's just not the same.

1. Mash the ricotta, Parmesan, herbs, and salt together in a medium-sized bowl using a fork or the back of a wooden spoon and set aside. The consistency of the mix should turn out like a paste; add a light splash of milk to thin out very dry ricotta, if needed, or squeeze the mixture through a piece of cheesecloth if it is runny.

2. In a second bowl, whip the sparkling water and flour.

3. Gently pry apart the flower petals and spoon or pipe about 1 teaspoon of the cheese mix into the open cavity. Use your fingers to push it in around the pistil; some recipes omit this step for space, but I like the crunchiness of it. Twist the petals to close.

4. Heat ¼ inch oil in a medium saucepan over medium heat. Holding the stem, gently dip and twist a flower in the batter until it is completely coated. Hold it over the bowl for a moment to allow some of the excess batter to run off before delicately sliding it into the hot oil.

5. Fry several blossoms at a time for about 3 minutes, or until all sides are crispy and golden brown.

6. Transfer individually to a pile of paper towels to soak up excess oil. Season to taste and serve.

Herb-Encrusted Goat Cheese

Ingredients

2 tablespoons finely chopped fresh chives

2 tablespoons finely chopped fresh parsley

2 tablespoons finely chopped fresh lemon thyme

140-gram log (5 ounces) chèvre (soft unripened goat's milk cheese)

Serves 3–4

You can buy shrink-wrapped herb-encrusted goat cheese in stores, but you'll pay a premium if the herbs are fresh because they don't last long on the shelf. Making your own takes a few minutes tops, and it tastes better than packaged. Serve it on a cheese plate with slices of fresh baguette, crostini, crackers, or Flowerpot Cornbread (page 158) and a spoonful of herb-infused honey (page 188). Simple, yet fancy.

1. In a small bowl, combine the herbs thoroughly.

2. Divide the log into three equally sized pieces and roll each piece in your hands to make small balls.

3. Roll the balls in the fresh herb mix, pressing to set the herbs into the cheese.

Flowerpot Cornbread

Ingredients

1½ cups cornmeal

1 cup flour

½ teaspoon sea salt

1 tablespoon baking powder

1 teaspoon finely chopped fresh sage leaves

1 tablespoon finely chopped fresh chives

1 large egg

1 cup buttermilk

3 tablespoons unsalted butter, softened

2 tablespoons grated Parmesan cheese (optional)

3 whole fresh sage leaves (optional)

Makes 3 loaves

These little cornbread loaves are simple but make a big impression on the table. For individually sized loaves, use smaller pots and fill to within an inch or two of the top with batter.

1. Preheat the oven to 400°F. Combine the cornmeal, flour, salt, baking powder, sage, and chives in a large mixing bowl. Make a well in the center.

2. In a medium bowl, beat the egg, buttermilk, and butter together, then pour into the dry ingredients and mix well until combined.

3. Coat the insides of the terra-cotta pots with olive oil, then center a 2 × 13-inch strip of parchment paper inside each pot so that it covers the hole. Hang the excess length over the sides and use as handles to remove the loaf later.

4. Divide the batter among all three pots. Sprinkle each loaf with an equal portion of Parmesan and garnish with a fresh sage leaf, if desired. Bake until golden brown or until a wooden skewer inserted into the center of the loaf comes out dry, 30–40 minutes. Set aside to cool for 5–10 minutes, then run a knife around the inside edge of the pot to loosen the loaf and pull on the parchment handles to help remove it.

VARIATIONS

A variety of herb combinations taste great in cornbread—don't be afraid to use whatever is in season or on hand, including green garlic, garlic scapes, marjoram, thyme, parsley, garlic chives, or lovage. Save prep time by adding a dollop of premade pesto (page 202) in place of chopped herbs.

Combine chili flakes, garlic, and onion greens for a Mexican-inspired loaf.

NOTE: Serve warm with Herbed Butters (page 182) or Herb-Encrusted Goat Cheese (page 157).

PREPARING THE POTS: You'll need to season or temper your terra-cotta before use. Seasoning creates a natural nonstick surface that makes it easy to remove the bread after baking. It's a time-consuming but essential process, and seasoned pots can be wiped clean and reused again and again.

- Wash three brand new, all-natural terra-cotta pots (4" tall × 4" at the top) in warm and soapy water and set aside to drip-dry.
- Thoroughly coat the inside of each pot with olive oil, making sure to get into all of the nooks and crannies.
- Place the pots in a cold oven and heat at 375°F for 20 minutes.
- Repeat steps 2 and 3 a few more times, allowing the pots to cool down in between.

Sorrel and Potato Soup

Ingredients

1 small onion, chopped

2 leeks (white and light green parts), thinly sliced

2 tablespoons butter

1 tablespoon olive oil

1 pound potatoes (peeled or unpeeled), diced

4 cups vegetable or chicken broth or water

4 cups roughly chopped fresh sorrel leaves

1 cup milk

Sea salt and pepper to taste

½ cup thick, plain yogurt (optional)

1 tablespoon chopped fresh chives (optional)

1 tuberous begonia flower (optional)

Serves 4

My version of this Eastern European favorite has a tangy sorrel bite that is preserved by adding the leaves in during the last few minutes of cooking. Serve it hot or cold like vichyssoise—don't leave out the yogurt!

1. In a large saucepan over medium-low heat, slowly sweat the onion and leeks in the butter and oil until soft and translucent, about 10 minutes.

2. Add the potatoes and broth. Bring to a boil, then reduce the heat and simmer with the lid on until the potatoes are very soft, about 20 minutes.

3. Add the sorrel leaves and cook for another minute or so until they are thoroughly wilted.

4. Turn the heat off and purée the soup with an immersion blender. Raise the heat to medium-low and stir in the milk.

5. Season to taste. Serve with a dollop of yogurt, chopped chives, and a few colorful tuberous begonia petals as garnish in each bowl, if desired.

Ramekin Frittatas

Ingredients

Small pat unsalted butter for ramekins

1 tablespoon flour

6 large eggs

2 tablespoons milk or cream

1 tablespoon roughly chopped fresh French tarragon leaves

1 tablespoon finely chopped fresh chives

Sea salt and black pepper to taste

4 squash flowers

½ cup ricotta cheese

Generous handful of arugula, washed and patted dry (optional)

Serves 4

These individually sized frittatas make a simple yet impressive weekend brunch. Leave out the squash flowers in the off-season or substitute thin zucchini slices instead.

1. Preheat the oven to 375°F. Lightly butter and flour four small ramekins.

2. In a medium bowl, whisk together the eggs and milk. Add the chopped herbs, season with salt and pepper, and stir to combine.

3. Divide the mixture among the ramekins and gently place one squash flower on top of each, along with a generous dollop of ricotta.

4. Bake for about 20 minutes, or until the frittatas are golden brown and the sides pull away with gentle coaxing.

5. Remove the frittatas and serve warm on a bed of arugula, if desired, with a spoonful of Mixed-Herb Coulis (page 203).

VARIATIONS

Substitute the fresh tarragon with other herbs you happen to have on hand. Basil, chive flowers, garlic chives, parsley, chervil, and Mexican tarragon are good options. You may need to reduce the quantity of sage, thyme, marjoram, Cuban oregano, or other strongly flavored herbs.

Herbal Salads

Both potted and in-ground gardens are brimming with seasonal salad fixings that are ready for harvest in the very early spring and continuing right through the winter in temperate climates. Choices range from the usual suspects—mild leafy greens, colorful lettuces, and arugula—to weeds like orache, chickweed, and purslane that may have been right under your feet all along.

Combining Herbs

1. For a balanced salad, use mild leaves to make up the bulk and accent with a smaller portion of the weird and wild possibilities that are so often overlooked in commercially prepared salad mixes. Tear a few basil, cress, sorrel, or nasturtium leaves into the mix or punctuate with colorful (but relatively tasteless) sweet violets, pansies, violas, and sunflower petals.

2. On the other hand, some flowers have very distinctive, strong flavors and should be used sparingly to avoid overpowering the salad. These include calendula, chives, French marigold, tuberous begonia, and bee balm. Nasturtium, borage, basil, and clove pinks lie somewhere in between, with distinctive, sometimes spicy flavors that can work in larger quantities and even as the main attraction. 'Scarlet Runner' bean flowers are one of my favorite examples of this. Their delicate, hint-of-bean taste and vibrant color make them an excellent flavor accent when you don't want to eat a pile of beans.

Salad Herbs

Angelica (young leaves)

Arugula

Basil

Bloody dock

Borage (young leaves and sprouts)

Bronze fennel

Calendula (young leaves)

Chervil

Chives

Cilantro

Claytonia, aka miner's lettuce

Cress

Dandelion (young leaves)

Dill

Fennel

Garlic chives

Green garlic (young leaves)

Lemon balm

Marjoram

Mint

Mustard greens

Nasturtium (leaves)

Orache

Oregano

Parsley

Purslane

Salad burnet

Savory (summer and winter)

Scallions (greens)

Sorrel

Tarragon

Violets (young leaves)

Watercress

Salad Flowers

Arugula

Basil

Bee balm

Borage

Broccoli

Calendula

Chamomile

Chives

Dandelion

Dianthus, aka clove pinks

Dill

Fennel

French marigold

Fruit sage

Gem Series marigolds

Mustard

Nasturtium

Pansy

Primrose

Radish

Roselle (*Hibiscus sabdariffa*)

Rose petals

Runner beans

Sage

Scented geranium

Signet marigold

Tuberous begonia

Viola

Violet

Lavender Shortbread

Ingredients

½ cup granulated sugar

1 tablespoon fresh lavender blossoms

1 cup cold unsalted butter

2 cups flour

Makes 32 cookies

When it comes to herbal shortbreads, lavender is a classic—and for good reason! Try this recipe first and then skip to the end and take a stab at some unusual herbal variations. If you have some on hand, use $\frac{1}{2}$ cup plus 1 tablespoon Lavender Blossom Sugar (page 200) in place of the sugar and fresh lavender blossoms.

1. Chop the sugar and lavender blossoms together in a food processor until they are finely ground.

2. In a mixing bowl, combine the lavender sugar and the butter until smooth.

3. Add the flour and mix to form a dough ball.

4. Divide the dough in half and press into two roughly shaped squares, about 1 inch thick. Cover each square in plastic wrap (clean, used plastic bags work well, too) and place the dough in the fridge to chill for 30 minutes.

5. Preheat the oven to 300°F and line a baking sheet with a silicone baking mat or parchment paper.

6. Unwrap the first square of dough and turn it onto an unfloured work surface. Press and roll the dough to form a 6 × 6-inch square (about ¼–½ inch thick). Divide with a sharp knife into 1½ × 1½-inch squares (four across and four down). Make three marks with a fork on each cookie and space the cookies evenly on the baking sheet.

7. Repeat with the second square of dough and place the cookies back in the fridge to chill until the oven is heated.

8. Bake for 20 to 30 minutes, or until the shortbreads are golden brown.

VARIATIONS

Because butter goes with everything, why not try a range of fresh and dried herbs in place of the lavender? Substitute 2 teaspoons finely chopped fresh lemon verbena, chamomile, rose geranium flowers, anise hyssop blossoms, or bee balm. Create sweet and savory cookies using 2 teaspoons sage, rosemary, or lemon thyme.

Salted Rosemary and Orange Shortbread

Substitute 1½ teaspoons finely chopped fresh rosemary and 1 teaspoon orange zest for the lavender. Sprinkle the tops of the cookies sparingly with coarse sea salt and serve alongside a scoop of Orange Rosemary and Honey Ice Cream (page 166).

Orange Rosemary and Honey Ice Cream

Ingredients

1¼ cups milk

2 teaspoons finely chopped fresh rosemary leaves

1 teaspoon orange zest

4 egg yolks

¼ cup honey

Juice of 1 orange

½ cup whipping cream

Serves 4–6

Ice cream is quite easy to make at home, even without a special machine. It's worth the effort, because chances are great you won't find a flavor like this one in your grocer's freezer.

I suggest serving a scoop alongside sliced or grilled peaches—the combination is delicious. If you prefer, you can also try stirring a cup of cooked or puréed fruit right into the custard before freezing.

1. Heat the milk over medium-low heat until just before the boiling point. You'll start to see a bit of frothing along the edges. Reduce the heat to low.

2. Stir the rosemary and orange zest into the milk and let it simmer for another minute.

3. Take the pan off the heat and let the flavors infuse into the milk for about 1 hour.

4. Lightly beat the eggs and honey together in a large bowl. Strain the infused milk into the egg-honey mixture, pressing down on the herbs with a wooden spoon to get every last drop of flavor out. Stir to combine.

5. Set the bowl over a pot of simmering water to create a double boiler. Stir the mixture constantly with a wooden spoon. You'll know it's ready when you can coat the back of the spoon with the custard and draw a line through it with your finger. This usually takes about 10 minutes.

6. Remove the bowl from the pan and allow it to cool down thoroughly. Keep stirring while it is hot to prevent curdling.

7. Lightly beat the orange juice and whipping cream together before mixing it into the custard. Pour the contents into an ice cream machine. If you don't have one, pour into a plastic bowl and freeze for about 1 hour. Stir it up and return it to the freezer. Keep checking and stirring every hour until it is completely frozen.

'Cinnamon' Basil Ice Cream: Substitute the herbs with 1 cup 'Cinnamon' basil or another variety such as 'Thai', 'Lemon', or even regular 'Genovese'. Omit the citrus to make the basil the star.

Rose petal, rose geranium, lavender blossoms, fennel, tarragon, and thyme are fun and delicious flavors to explore.

Switch Up the Sweetener

Switch out the honey for an equal measure of herbed sugar. (See page 200 for recipes). For a more intense flavor, infuse the honey with rosemary leaves or flowers a few days before making the ice cream (pages 188–189).

Homegrown Bloody Mary Mix

Ingredients

1 pound ripe medium tomatoes

Small handful of fresh basil leaves

Sea salt and cracked black pepper to taste

2 thick stalks fresh lovage

Cucumber slices and/or cherry tomatoes for garnish (optional)

¾ cup Spicy Basil-Infused Vodka (page 191)

1½ tablespoons lemon juice

1½ tablespoons lime juice

1 teaspoon Worcestershire sauce, or to taste

Ice

Serves 4

Of course you can make this drink by substituting commercially produced tomato juice, but do yourself a favor and give it a whirl using fresh tomatoes when they're in season. It turns out so sweet and yummy you will run your finger along the inside of the glass to scoop up those last vestiges of flavor. I do!

1. For the tomato juice base: Purée the tomatoes and basil in a food processor or blender and press through a sieve to remove the skins and solids. Alternatively, press through a food mill or an old-fashioned chinois.

2. Season with sea salt and black pepper and set in the fridge to chill for 30–60 minutes.

3. For the Bloody Marys: Snip the leaves off the stalks of lovage and cut each stalk into two approximately 6-inch edible straws. Prepare four toothpicks or wooden skewers with two cherry tomatoes and a cucumber slice each, if desired.

4. In a pitcher, mix together the seasoned tomato juice, vodka, lemon juice, lime juice, and Worcestershire sauce.

5. To serve, fill each glass with ice and Bloody Mary mix. Garnish with the tomato/cucumber skewers, if using, and an edible lovage straw. You'll taste a hint of lovage as you sip through it. Cheers!

VARIATIONS

Before filling individual glasses with ice, wet the rims with a piece of lemon and dip into a mix of dried basil and sea salt.

Herbal Citrus-Ades

Serves 5–6

A tall, icy glass of lemonade or limeade is a nice way to cool down on a scorching hot day. Infusing fresh or dried herbs into these classic summer drinks adds depth and character and surely increases their monetary value at the sidewalk lemonade stand.

Pink Lemonade
Makes 5–6 cups

1. In a mug or small teapot, steep the herbs and hibiscus flowers in 1½ cups hot water for 5–10 minutes. Hibiscus flowers are optional, as they amplify the bright pink color and only add a hint of flavor.

2. Strain out the herbs and dissolve the honey while the brew is still warm.

3. Add the lemon juice to a large pitcher along with the sweetened herbal tea.

4. Stir in 4 cups cold, filtered water and serve with lots of crushed or cubed ice.

5. Garnish with fresh herbs and sliced citrus.

NOTE: When using dried herbs in place of fresh, reduce the quantity by half.

Mint Limeade
Makes 5–6 cups

1. Repeat the directions for making Pink Lemonade (above), using fresh mint in place of the listed herbs and lime juice instead of lemon juice. Omit the hibiscus flowers.

2. Garnish with fresh mint flowers or leaves and sliced limes.

Ingredients

1 tablespoon roughly chopped fresh lemon verbena leaves

2 tablespoons lavender blossoms

2 hibiscus flowers (optional)

½ cup honey, or to taste

1 cup lemon juice

1 cup (packed) fresh mint

¼ cup Mint-Infused Honey (page 189), or to taste

½ cup lime juice (from about 4 limes)

VARIATIONS

Turn these into herbal citrus sodas by replacing the flat water with sparkling, bottled water.

Sweeten with your choice of granulated sugar (try one of the herbed sugars on page 200), maple syrup, or agave syrup.

Citrus Cocktails

In a freezer-safe container, mix Mint Limeade with several shots of tequila and pop it in the freezer for an instant frozen margarita mix.

A splash or two of gin or bourbon turns Pink Lemonade into something slightly sinful.

Hibiscus Punch

Ingredients

1 cup hibiscus calyces (dried or fresh)

1 tablespoon roughly chopped fresh ginger

One 3-inch cinnamon stick

1 tablespoon cane sugar, honey, or agave syrup (optional)

Makes 4–5 cups

Latin Americans refer to this beverage as *agua de Jamaica* and West Indians call it *sorrel*, although it is made with vibrantly colored hibiscus flowers and has no relation to the hardy French herb.

Whatever you choose to call it, this drink is remarkably thirst-quenching on a scorching day. Spike it with a shot of Hibiscus Bush Rum (page 191) and enjoy a cheery holiday punch, Caribbean style.

1. Steep the hibiscus calyces, ginger, cinnamon stick, and sweetener (if using) in 4 cups hot water for several hours.

2. Once cooled, place in the fridge and continue to steep for as little or as long as you prefer. Taste it as you go—I like mine at the end of two days.

3. Strain and serve with a heap of crushed or cubed ice.

VARIATIONS

For a healthier version, cut the sweetener completely. This is how we make it at home—adding the cinnamon stick (a secret I gleaned by drinking countless glasses in the West Indies) brightens and even sweetens the taste naturally.

Create your own riffs on this recipe by substituting some of the water with sparkling water (we love this) or adding orange zest, 'Cinnamon' basil, cloves, stevia, or lime juice.

CHAPTER 11

Growing the Pantry: Preserving and Storing Herbs

Preparing and preserving your own homegrown herbs for future usage is joyful, optimistic handiwork. Plucking fresh basil leaves off stems, chopping handfuls of parsley for freezing, and bundling up sprigs of aromatic oregano to hang are the sort of satisfying, prideful tasks you can do with the music blaring and a dance in your step, knowing that all of this good stuff you grew yourself is going to make a reappearance well after the fresh stuff is long gone.

Every jar of mint syrup and every batch of frozen homegrown pesto is money in the bank . . . and it smells so good while you do it, too. I always feel happy and alive through this part of the process, even when the floor is covered in leaves and scraps and I know there is no way I can possibly get through it all before midnight.

Short-Term Storage

I never seem to get around to using freshly picked herbs as quickly as I intend to. Herbs are always at their best right after picking, but most will maintain their integrity for at least a few days if you take a moment directly after picking to attend to their needs appropriately.

Sprigs or stems of fresh oregano, marjoram, tarragon, cilantro, mint, calendula, lemon balm, and nasturtium last days on the counter in a vase of fresh water like a leafy bouquet. This is also the very best way to keep cold-sensitive herbs like basil and lemon verbena that will turn black and rot almost immediately if placed in the fridge.

Parsley, lovage, thyme, and chives, on the other hand, seem to prefer being wrapped in a moist cloth or paper towel and set in the drawer compartment of the fridge. They tend to go yellow very quickly if left on the counter.

Individual flower heads and petals store really well in a glass Mason or canning jar (with a glass top) when placed in the fridge. Don't lock the lid down tightly with clamps or a screw top. Instead, leave a bit of room to breathe. A small piece of wet cheesecloth or paper towel in the bottom helps retain moisture but isn't always necessary.

Save Paper Towels

Keep washcloths, cheesecloth, and small pieces of old kitchen towel on hand for wrapping up herbs and a few 5″ × 5″ bits for placing in the bottom of glass storage jars. Wash and use them again and again.

I've kept roses, nasturtiums, dianthus, daylilies, pansies, and violets for unbelievable stretches of time in this way, and even zucchini blossoms that never last more than a day by other methods just keep going and going in a glass container. Small pieces of leafy herbs like this treatment, too.

Prechopped leaves start to degrade immediately and can go moldy in a heartbeat. I don't recommend storing them for longer than a day, but if you can't bear to part with them, try keeping them in a bowl or cup with a blanket of moist cloth draped on top so that the leaves get some air but don't lose their moisture.

Herbal Infusions

Oils, fats, sugar syrups, vinegar, and alcohol have a long history as both delivery vehicles for capturing the essence of freshly picked herbs and as preservatives that will keep them around longer than would be possible without the aid of a fridge or freezer. The high acid content of vinegar keeps botulism at bay, and high-proof alcohol is a pickling liquid of another sort. They both have a reasonable shelf life. Sweet liquids such as honey and simple syrup that are low in water content will last a while in the cupboard or the fridge, but oils are no longer considered safe for preserving on their own. They tend to go rancid and can act as a petri dish for harmful microorganisms in our warm, modern houses. For that reason they should always be refrigerated or frozen and never left out on the counter for even a short period of time.

The following preserving recipes will give you plenty of options for making meals sing even after fresh herbs are no longer at your fingertips.

Pickled Green Coriander Seeds

Ingredients

½ cup fresh green coriander seeds

Zest and juice of ½ lemon

¼ teaspoon coarse salt

1 garlic clove

1 or 2 small hot or mild peppers

1 cup wine vinegar

NOTE: Stick to using a stainless steel or glass pot because vinegar can react to some metals.

Makes ½ pint

Green, undeveloped coriander seeds are an herbal delicacy only gardeners have access to. The flavor is more intensely aromatic than in the mature seeds and delivers a strong citrus burst when you bite into them. Release the flavor by crushing with the back of a knife before serving fresh alongside smoked salmon or in summer salads. They'll work just about anywhere you would typically use capers. They will keep in the fridge for several months.

1. Pack the coriander seeds, lemon zest and juice, salt, garlic, and peppers into a clean glass jar.

2. In a medium stainless steel saucepan, simmer the vinegar over medium-low heat so that it is warm but not boiling. Pour the vinegar into the jar over the coriander seed mixture and let it cool completely.

3. Once cool, place the jar in the fridge to steep and mellow out for 1–2 weeks. Of course, no one is stopping you from using the seeds within a day if you can't wait.

VARIATION

To make a spicier pickle, cut the hot peppers open before adding them to the jar.

Chive Blossom Vinegar

Ingredients

1 cup chive blossoms

1 cup white wine or white vinegar

Makes 1 cup

Chive blossoms are a short-term crop that come and go in the spring before you can bat an eyelash. Capturing their mild chive flavor in a good-quality vinegar is the perfect way to enjoy them well past their season.

1. Harvest the chive blossoms in the spring just after they open. To prepare the chive blossoms, snip off the stems and gently jostle them in a bowl of cool water to remove all dirt and debris. Pile the wet blossoms into the center of a clean, dry kitchen towel, pull up all of the corners to create a sack, and shake vigorously until the blossoms are dry.

2. Stuff a clean pint-sized Mason jar with the clean blossoms.

3. In a small saucepan, gently warm the vinegar over medium-low heat. Do not bring to a boil. Pour the vinegar over the blossoms, making sure to submerge them completely.

4. Once the liquid has cooled, cover the jar with a lid made of nonreactive material such as glass. Alternatively, protect a metal canning lid by first placing a square of waxed paper between the jar and the lid.

5. Store in a cool, dark cupboard for a week or two and strain into a second, clean or sterilized jar when the vinegar suits your taste buds.

VARIATIONS

Frankly, all herbal vinegars are delicious—experiment with several edible flowers, leaves, and seeds and keep a medley of flavors on hand.

Sterilize the jar if you intend to keep the vinegar for a month or more. Otherwise, store it in the fridge for short-term usage. To sterilize, heat the jar in the oven for 20 minutes at 250°F.

Basil-Infused Olive Oil

Ingredients

2 cups (packed) fresh basil leaves

1 cup good quality extra-virgin olive oil

Makes 1 cup

Infusing extra-virgin olive oil with intense, freshly chopped basil, oregano, sage, rosemary, citrus peel, or lavender is a different way to introduce herb flavoring to a dish. Infused oils are a natural for cold salad dressings or when pan-frying, but you can also drizzle a little over a plate of cooked pasta, eggs, vegetables, fish dishes, and soups as a final, flavorful garnish, or serve them as the Italians do as a dip for chunks of good bread.

Serve this concoction on homegrown summer tomatoes with chunks of fresh mozzarella and a dash of balsamic vinegar. Use it as a marinade for grilled vegetables, as a "wash" before grilling bread in a panini maker, or as the base oil for basil-flavored aïoli. This oil's potential is practically limitless.

NOTE: Unfortunately, infused oils have a very short shelf life. Using fresh herbs introduces moisture to the oil that can cause spoilage or even lead to botulism. Always keep infused oils refrigerated and use within a week. Never leave them out on the counter for long periods of time.

1. Blanch the basil leaves in a pot of boiling water for just a few seconds, then scoop them out and quickly plunge into icy cold water. Soft-leaved herbs such as basil, chervil, mint, and chives require blanching to help retain their color and coax out their flavor.

2. Squeeze as much moisture as you can out of the basil using your hands or a clean kitchen towel.

3. Purée the basil and oil in a blender and strain through a fine-mesh sieve or cheesecloth into a clean glass Mason jar.

VARIATIONS

Oils flavored with sage, rosemary, oregano, lavender blossoms, and other resinous herbs are particularly easy to make, as the leaves are tough and stand up well to heating. Lightly heat 1 cup oil over low heat, then turn off the heat and add $1/2$ cup chopped and smashed fresh herbs. Allow the infusion to steep for 30 minutes and pour through a sieve into a clean glass jar. Sage oil is particularly warming and delicious drizzled onto pumpkin or squash soup. Serve rosemary or lavender oil with baked potatoes.

Herbed Butters

Makes about ½ cup
Don't be afraid to experiment with using different herbal combinations here—several follow, but you really can't go wrong when the main ingredient is butter.

1. Set the butter aside to soften.

2. Wash, dry, chop, and assemble the herbs required for the chosen recipe.

3. Stir all of the ingredients together in a bowl until thoroughly mixed.

4. Shape into balls or logs, or press into a small bowl. Set the butter in the fridge for 30 minutes to harden. Wrap small chunks in parchment paper and store in freezer bags for a few months.

Variations to Try
Calendula petals

Chive or chive flower

Cilantro

Cress

Lemon thyme

Nasturtium

Parsley

Rosemary

Rose petals

Sage flowers

Violet flowers

½ cup unsalted butter, softened

2 tablespoons finely chopped fresh tarragon

1 teaspoon finely grated lemon zest

½ teaspoon sea salt

Tarragon Butter

If you can, make tarragon butter early in the season when the leaves are soft and delicate. It's not quite as sweet later on once they've toughened up a bit.

½ cup unsalted butter, softened

4 tablespoons finely chopped fresh basil leaves

1 garlic clove

Fresh ground black pepper to taste

Basil Butter

'Genovese' basil makes the most pesto-like version, but colorful varieties like 'Dark Opal' and 'Siam Queen' infuse a bright hue through the butter along with their flavor.

½ cup unsalted butter, softened

2 tablespoons finely chopped sage leaves

1 tablespoon finely chopped shallot

¼ teaspoon sea salt

Sage Butter

Sage always seems to be at its best when served with melt-in-your-mouth mashed sweet potatoes, roasted turkey, pumpkin ravioli, and other foods from the harvest season. It's also really yummy slathered on baked potatoes and grilled corn on the cob, but then again, what isn't? When they're in season, substitute sage flowers for the leaves.

½ cup unsalted butter, softened

1 tablespoon lavender flowers, finely chopped

1 tablespoon honey

1 teaspoon finely grated orange zest

Honey-Lavender Butter

This combination of floral sweetness and fat is especially sumptuous on a slice of warm bread or melting between the top and bottom of a muffin.

Mint Syrup

Ingredients

2 cups (tightly packed) fresh mint leaves

1 cup granulated cane sugar

1 tablespoon bottled lemon juice

Makes about 2½ cups

This recipe is a saving grace come midsummer when I am saddled with a sack of fresh mint and the dilemma of how to capture its fresh flavor quickly before it rots on my kitchen counter.

Macerating and steeping the mint in the sugar is a step beyond the typical simple syrup recipe, but it's worth the extra effort. The result is a much more intensely flavored, rich syrup that you can use to sweeten pancakes, as a dessert topping, or to flavor sparkling wine, prosecco, and a myriad of other alcoholic beverages. Use it as a sweetener for cold sweet tea or lemonade. Thin it out with water or sparkling water to make Italian sodas, herbal granitas (page 186), or ice pops.

1. Tear or chop the mint leaves and add them to a bowl along with the sugar and lemon juice, and ¼ cup boiling water. Crush the leaves into the sugar by pounding for a minute or two with a wooden pestle, a muddler, or the end of a rolling pin. (The smells you'll encounter during this process are incredible and will clear out your sinuses!)

2. Cover the bowl with a plate and set aside for 2–8 hours so that the mint essence can infuse into the sugar. The longer you leave it, the more intense the infusion will be.

3. Pour 2 cups boiling water over the mixture and stir well, scraping down the sides to liquefy the grains of sugar that have settled around the bowl. Set aside to steep for a few minutes more.

4. While the mint is steeping, wash 5 half-pint Mason jars in warm soapy water and set aside to drip-dry. Set the dry jars on a baking pan and sterilize them in the oven for 20 minutes at 250°F.

5. Strain the liquefied sugar-mint mixture through a fine sieve into a medium saucepan. Push down on the mint with the back of a wooden spoon to extract all of the liquid.

Other Syrup Infusions

Anise hyssop

Basil (sweet, lemon, cinnamon, anise)

Bronze fennel

Citrus zest

Ginger

Hibiscus flowers

Lavender blossoms

Lemon balm

Lemongrass

'Lemon' thyme

Lemon verbena

Rosemary

Rose petals

Sage

Shiso

Violet flowers

6. Gently simmer over medium-low heat, stirring until the sugar grains have completely dissolved. Raise the heat to medium and bring to a boil, stirring continuously to prevent the syrup from burning on the bottom of the pan. Continue boiling vigorously for 2 minutes, then remove from the heat immediately.

7. Pour the warm liquid into sterilized jars and set them on a wooden surface or kitchen towel to cool. Once the jars have cooled to room temperature, store them in the fridge for several months. It is not unusual to find little bits of herb floating in the jar. Stir or shake before use.

NOTE: For long-term shelf storage, pour into sterilized Mason jars, leaving ¼ inch headspace, and heat-process in a boiling-water bath for 10 minutes. Keep in the fridge once opened.

Herbal Happy Hour

Herbal spritzers are a cheap and cheerful way to give a second life to a bottle of humdrum wine. Add 1 or 2 tablespoons of the herbal syrup of your choice to a tall glass of ice. Fill the glass to the halfway mark with white wine (Riesling and Pinot Grigio are good choices) and top with sparkling water.

Mint and White Wine Granita

Ingredients

¼ cup Mint Syrup
(page 184)

½ cup white wine

1 teaspoon lemon juice

Serves 2

Don't be intimidated by the word *granita*—it's really just a fancy, adult take on the drink-mix slushies we made as kids. For a nonalcoholic version, substitute sparkling water for the wine.

1. Mix the syrup, white wine, lemon juice, and ½ cup cold water together in a wide plastic or freezer-safe container with a watertight lid. Shallow pans with a wide surface area freeze faster but become a spill hazard in an overfilled freezer.

2. Freeze the mixture for a few hours, stirring every hour or so with a fork to keep it from forming into a solid block. A timer set to the hour really helps here.

3. If the granita does freeze completely, set the container out to thaw slightly for about 20 minutes before serving.

4. Scrape with a fork to break the ice up into chips and serve immediately.

VARIATIONS

Syrup or honey (page 189) infused with rose petals, lemon verbena, anise hyssop, lemon balm, or lemon basil is delicious in place of mint syrup.

Rose Petal–Infused Honey

Ingredients

1 cup wildflower honey

3 cups (packed) fresh rose petals

Makes 1 cup

Like fine wine, honey flavors vary from region to region and year to year depending on growing conditions and the flowers the bees feed on. I didn't come to appreciate this complexity until I started infusing my honey with homegrown herbs and flowers. Now I always have several different types on hand—I match different honeys to complementary herbs and use the final result to alter the taste of tea and lemonade and to sweeten desserts. I like the floral flavors on my morning yogurt or served with good cheese.

Honey takes on the medicinal properties of each herb as well as its flavor. Be patient and keep the temperature very low when heating; otherwise you risk destroying the honey's natural enzymes.

1. In a double boiler, heat the honey and rose petals for 15 minutes over very low heat, stirring constantly. If you do not have a double boiler, set a heatproof bowl inside a small pot of water.

2. Pour the honey-flower mixture into a clean jar and store in a dark place to continue steeping. Infuse mild herbs like rose petals for up to several weeks, and very strong herbs such as rosemary, sage, or wild bergamot for just a few days. Taste the honey every few days to test the strength of the infusion. It's really all a matter of personal taste.

3. When the desired strength is reached, strain the honey into a second, clean jar.

Other Herbs to Try

Flowers

Anise hyssop

Chamomile

Hibiscus

Lavender

Lemon verbena

Marjoram

Mint

Rose geranium

Rose petals

Sage

Thyme

Wild bergamot

Leaves

Anise hyssop

Lemon balm

Lemon verbena

Mint (peppermint, applemint, 'Chocolate', 'Ginger')

Rosemary

Sage

Thyme

Seeds and Roots

Coriander

Ginger

Lemongrass

No-Mess Version

Planning to flavor an entire jar of honey? Save the effort of wrangling a gooey mess and just stick the glass jar into a pot of warm water rather than emptying the contents into a double boiler. Add the herbs to the jar, push them down into the honey with a chopstick, and you're done. Don't do this when the jar is plastic.

VARIATIONS

Rose Geranium Honey

1 cup wildflower honey

½ cup rose geranium flowers

2 rose geranium leaves, roughly chopped

Lavender Blossom Honey

1 cup wildflower honey

¼ cup lavender blossoms

Mint-Infused Honey

1 cup wildflower honey

2–4 tablespoons finely chopped fresh mint (leaves and flowers)

Bush Booze

I was first introduced to the concept of herb-infused alcohol on a trip to Dominica, a small island in the Caribbean (my maternal family comes from there). Those with an iron gut drink "bush rum," a very high-proof cane rum infused with herbs, fruit, spices, and other oddities—including meat! Bush is a colloquial term for herbs but also refers to the clandestine way this herbal hooch is prepared, sold, and consumed.

My experimental bush booze is decidedly less powerful than the original inspiration and a lot more drinkable by my standards. A remarkable range of herbs can be used to make delicious aperitifs—don't be afraid to experiment! I've personally tried dozens of herbs, and some of the most unexpected flavors (coriander, lovage, and dill) have turned out to be favorites. Even when they don't work on their own, the herb-infused spirits can always be saved for deglazing a cooking pan or flavoring a hearty stew.

Use the following recipes as a base ingredient for mixed drinks or serve ice-cold and straight up in shot-sized sipping glasses as an aperitif. No matter the season, these herbal infusions go down smooth and warm the belly like a tonic.

To make the booze:

1. Add all ingredients to a clean jar. Pour alcohol on top to cover.

2. Steep in a cool, dark place for 1 day to a week. Use your taste buds and intuition to adjust the steeping time and amount used. Don't leave the herbs in indefinitely—they turn bitter over time.

3. Strain out the herbs and use the infused alcohol as required.

NOTE: The labels shown in the photo (opposite) are available for download online at easy-growing.com. Print them out and affix to recycled glass bottles.

Spicy Basil-Infused Vodka

750 milliliters vodka

1 cup roughly chopped
fresh 'Purple Ruffles' basil

2 garlic cloves

4 garlic chive leaves

1 hot pepper (optional)

Makes 3 cups

Drink this hot-or-not basil-infused vodka alone, or better yet, add it to homemade tomato juice for the best Bloody Mary ever (page 168). Steep for one day and keep tasting every day after that—it can go from balanced to overwhelming in no time.

Hibiscus Bush Rum

750 milliliters white rum

1 cup dried hibiscus calyces

Makes 3 cups

I prefer to use white rum instead of dark for this infusion because it is so easily dyed a nuclear red color by the hibiscus flowers. Serve it during the holiday season or at a red-themed party.

Green Fennel Seed Rum

375 milliliters white rum

1 large fennel seed head
with immature, green seeds

Makes 1½ cups

When making this drink, leave the seed head intact but lightly pound the seeds with a rolling pin to release their flavor before adding to the rum. This works really well with vodka, too. I can't decide which is better.

Drying Herbs

There are lots of ways to dry herbs and a variety of methods that suit different lifestyles. I have air-dried heaps of herbs in a tiny apartment for well over a decade without the aid of an oven, microwave, or electric dehydrator—you'll want to use one of those devices if you live in a humid climate or don't have the space to commit to air-drying. The aim is to dry the herbs thoroughly and as quickly as possible, before they lose those delicious, aromatic oils.

Some herbs take better to quick drying than others. Rosemary, lemon verbena, lovage, and basil leaves are just a few examples of herbs that dry effortlessly. I've dried several of these by accident, simply by forgetting to add more water to a vase or leaving them on a chopping board overnight.

Plants such as chervil, cilantro, chives, salad burnet, dill, and fennel dry easily but tend to lose their flavor and color through the drying process. Lower your expectations and use larger quantities in recipes to make up for their blandness or skip this method in favor of freezing.

Humidity is another important factor to consider, because too much moisture in the air encourages mold and severely impedes the drying process, regardless of the method used. Time large batch drying to correspond with the dry season or a short period of drought. Take advantage of a weekend baking session when the oven will be heating up the kitchen and move drying plants to that room of the house.

Regardless of the herb, and whether you are drying the leaves, roots, seeds, stems, or fruit, all herb bits should be crackling dry before storing them away. Vintage glass canning jars are great for storage, especially the hinged kind, as long as they are airtight. To maintain their flavor, color, and integrity, leave the herbs as whole as possible and wait to crush or grind them up finely just before use.

Air-Drying

Air-drying is the cheapest and most environmentally friendly way to go but also the slowest if conditions aren't right. Loosely tie up the stems of small bundles of herbs with twine and hang them to dry in warm (not hot), dark parts of the house where there is a bit of a breeze or decent airflow.

The best spot in my former, cramped apartment was the least obvious. I hung the herbs on a spring-loaded bar set across an underused doorway where there was excellent circulation but no light. Coat hangers are another cheap and easy hanging option. Separate the bundles by a few inches of space so there is room for air to flow around the stems.

Lay small clusters or individual leaves, seeds, flowers, or roots on top of newsprint or mesh screening so that they aren't touching or overlapping. Or you can get fancy and build a wooden drying cabinet with mesh screens at the bottom of each drawer to keep the light out but bring air in.

Oven and Microwave Drying

If you've got a regular-sized oven, save the drying for a big batch of herbs so you can make use of all of that space in one go. Countertop toaster ovens are perfect for small batches. The ideal drying temperature for most herbs is around 80–95°F, but since kitchen ovens don't go that low, you'll need to set yours at the lowest temperature and prop the door open slightly to prevent it from getting too hot. The key is removing water from the herb bits slowly to avoid cooking or baking the flavor right out. This can take 30 minutes or several hours, depending on the herb, so be sure to check on them regularly.

Microwaves dry herbs incredibly fast—a minute or two tops is all you need to zap leaves to a crisp.

Dehydrator Drying

Electric dehydrators are great when it is too humid to air dry effectively. They're not as hot as ovens and are better for doing smaller batches as your herbs come into season. When purchasing a dehydrator, look for a model that has an adjustable thermostat that goes down as low as 90–95°F and is not too noisy (this is key in an apartment). A high wattage capacity is important (mine is 700 watts) or else it will take forever to dry a simple mint leaf, and you also want one that has a top- or side-mounted fan so that wet herbs don't drip onto it.

Drying times vary depending on the machine and the herb; however, leaves usually take a couple of hours and fruit can take up to a few days. Chop roots into small chunks or thin slices to reduce drying times.

Tie up bundles of herbs right in the garden as you pick them and save yourself the hassle of sorting, bundling, and tying them later on.

Herbs That Dry Well

Leaves and Stems
Rosemary, sage, basil, lovage, savory, tarragon, thyme, parsley, lemon balm, lemon verbena, stevia, bay, lime.

Flowers
Chamomile, hibiscus, anise hyssop, lavender, fennel, marigold, borage, bee balm, calendula.

Remove stems and lay flat on a sheet of paper or mesh screen. Set in a dry place out of the sun for a few days to several weeks, until brittle.

HIBISCUS FLOWERS: Use the petals fresh and dry the calyx only. Strip off the calyces and lay flat to air-dry in the sun or in the oven.

Roots and Bulbs
Horseradish, onions, garlic, ginger.

Set the oven or dehydrator to a higher temperature than used for leaves or fruit (about 140°F).

Thin slices are easier to dry but lose their flavor faster. To preserve the best flavor and scent, dry in large pieces and grind fresh as you need it.

GARLIC: Tie up the stems and hang the bulbs to "cure" in a dry spot for several weeks. Trim the roots and cut the stems down to about an inch or so above the bulbs. Store in a cool, dark place—never in the fridge.

Seeds and Fruit
Fennel, coriander, caraway, anise, dill, lovage, rose hips.

Harvest long stems of dill, fennel, coriander, and so on with nearly ripened seeds and loosely tie them together into small bundles. Cover the seed heads with a paper bag and hang to dry. The seeds will fall into the bag as they mature, a process that can take a few days to a few weeks, depending on the plant and the drying conditions.

ROSE HIPS: Harvest ripe hips just after the first frost. Slice the stem and blossom ends off each hip and lay flat to air-dry, or use an oven or dehydrator set to the lowest temperature to avoid losing vitamin C. Alternately, slice each hip in half and scoop out the seeds and irritating fine hairs before drying. Large, fleshy hips can take a few weeks to air-dry and are wrinkly and hard when ready.

CHILI PEPPERS: To make your own chili flakes, hang whole, blemish-free peppers, or cut them in half and lay flat in a dehydrator set to 115°F. Drying time depends on the size of the pepper and the thickness of the flesh. Crush with a mortar and pestle when thoroughly dry.

SUNFLOWER SEEDS: Hang or lay whole heads out of the sun and separate the seeds as they come loose. Cover hanging heads with cheesecloth or loosely woven muslin to hold the drying seeds.

Dried Herbal Tisane Blends

Making herbal infusions, or tisanes as they are known in hoity-toity circles, is one of the simplest ways to use up the bounty from an overgrown garden. Even a few pots of mint will yield enough fresh leaves to enjoy through the summer and a small harvest to dry and keep you warm through the chilly months.

Lemon Rose

Serves 4

The high vitamin C content of the rose hips in this mix makes it an excellent winter tonic.

1 tablespoon dried lemon verbena leaves

1 tablespoon fresh or dried rosehips, crushed

2 tablespoons fresh or dried rose petals

Lemon Lavender Mint

Serves 6

Soothing and sedating with a hint of freshness from the mint.

2 tablespoons lavender blossoms

2 tablespoons lemon balm

2 tablespoons mint leaves

Bedtime Tea

Serves 6

The herbs in this mix are known for their ability to gently guide you into sleep at the end of a long, harried day.

4 tablespoons chamomile flowers

2 tablespoons 'Lemon' catnip

Fruity Mint

Serves 8

A bright, refreshing, and soothing mix for an autumn day.

4 tablespoons anise hyssop flowers

2 tablespoons lemon balm

2 tablespoons bee balm

1 tablespoon spearmint

Quick and Easy Tea Bags

Make It

Make these tea bags ahead of time and store in a glass jar for several months. Replicate expensive tea bags at a fraction of the cost by substituting the cheesecloth with clean sheer curtains or silk. Tie the bags with baker's twine or colorful embroidery thread.

You Will Need

Cheesecloth or muslin

8 feet baker's twine

1 to 2 cups Dried Herbal Tisane Blend (page 195)

1. Cut the cheesecloth into a dozen 6-inch squares and the string into 8-inch lengths.

2. Place 1 tablespoon of the herbal tisane blend of your choice in the center of each square and spread it around equally.

3. Fold the left and right sides to create a tube, then fold in half lengthwise, gathering the ends together to create a little bundle. Tie closed with a piece of baker's twine and trim off extra fabric from the top of the bundle with a pair of shears.

Making the Tea Tags
Download printable tea tag designs online at easy-growing.com. Alternatively, make your own tags using scrap paper cut into 2″ × 1″ pieces. Fold a tag in half over the loose end of a tea bag string and staple in place.

Tasty Tea Herbs

CITRUS/ACIDIC: Lemon verbena, lemon balm, lemon thyme, lemongrass, 'Lemon' basil, orange mint, coriander seed, rose hips, 'Lemon' catnip, hibiscus flowers, orange and lemon zest.

FRUITY: Apple mint, chamomile, rose hips, rose petals, pineapple sage.

MINT AND LICORICE: Peppermint, spearmint, anise hyssop, licorice root, bee balm, sweet cicely, fennel seed, aniseed.

AROMATIC: Garden sage, catnip, rosemary, lavender blossoms, oregano, dill seed.

HERBAL: Raspberry leaves, strawberry leaves, red clover (*Trifolium pratense*), yarrow, mullein.

SPICY: 'Cinnamon' basil, ginger, cinnamon bark, cloves, cardamom, star anise.

Sweetener in the Bag

Stevia is a South American herb that is 300 times sweeter than sugar, without the ill health effects. Add a tiny pinch to each tea bag before closing it up to make an all-in-one teabag that you can travel with.

Dried-Herb Blends

The last big harvest of the season can leave you with an overwhelming abundance of herbs. The following blends are classic combinations that you are bound to use over and over again throughout the winter. Premixing saves the hassle of measuring each out repeatedly.

Scarborough Fair Mix

4 tablespoons dried parsley

2 tablespoons dried rosemary

2 tablespoons dried sage

2 tablespoons dried lemon thyme

3 dried bay leaves, crushed

Serves 2–4

This combination, adapted from the famous ballad, makes an exceptional mix for Thanksgiving stuffing, whether vegan or bird. Depending on your climate and the occasion, you can also substitute fresh herbs, but if you do, double the quantity used.

Try to keep the leaves whole and intact if you can for storage purposes—they'll hold their flavor longer this way. Crush them with your fingers directly before use.

Salad Dressing Mix

2 tablespoons dried oregano

2 tablespoons dried 'Lemon' basil

2 tablespoons dried chervil

1 tablespoon dried marjoram

1 tablespoon dried mint

Serves 8

Add this mix to olive oil and vinegar for an easy winter herb dressing, or toss it onto salad greens straight up with your own choice of oil and a squeeze of lemon juice. Meyer lemon is even better!

To use this mix in a dressing, combine 1 tablespoon dried herb mix with 3 tablespoons olive oil, 1 tablespoon Chive Blossom Vinegar (page 178), 1 teaspoon honey, and a pinch of sea salt to taste. Let it sit for 15 minutes or so before serving to allow the herbs time to marinate in the liquid.

Pizza Topping

Serves 4–5

4 tablespoons dried oregano

4 tablespoons dried 'Dark Opal' basil

1 tablespoon dried thyme

1 tablespoon hot pepper flakes (optional)

Homemade pizza is a weekly event around here. This dried mix is a great way to add flavor in the last legs of winter when plain tomato sauce is all we've got left from the summer's preserves.

Sprinkle to taste into the sauce, onto the cheese, or better yet, right into the dough if you've got the ambition to make it from scratch. I am coming over.

1. Mix the dried herbs together in a bowl. Leave all seeds whole and try to avoid crushing the herbs until moments before use. This maintains the integrity of the flavor for a longer period of time.

2. Store loose in an airtight, glass container in a dark, dry place for up to a year. The kitchen cupboard farthest from the stove is a good option because there is less chance of subjecting the herbs to steam and heat.

Hearty Soup Mix

Makes 1 cup

4 tablespoons dried parsley

4 tablespoons dried basil

3 tablespoons dried chives

2 tablespoons dried savory

1 tablespoon dried marjoram

1 tablespoon dried thyme

1 tablespoon dried rosemary

3 dried bay leaves, crushed

This mix has a deep, intense flavor that is suited to winter broths and thick, stick-to-your-ribs bean soups. Stay warm.

SOUP AND STEW SACHETS: For the sake of convenience, prepackage mixes into homemade cloth tea bags and store them in a glass jar. When you're making a soup, sauce, or stew, simply reach for a bag in the cupboard and pop it open. A jar of organically grown herb sachets makes a very nice gift, too. I recently saw jars going for several dollars a piece at an upscale culinary boutique. Follow the directions for Dried Herbal Tisane Blends on page 195.

Lavender Blossom Sugar

Ingredients

2 cups sugar

⅓ cup (tightly packed) fresh or dried lavender buds

Variations

Substitute lavender with any of these herbs, using the same quantity as indicated in the recipe.

- Anise hyssop flowers
- Bronze fennel leaves
- 'Cinnamon' basil
- Citrus flowers
- Dianthus flowers
- Fennel seeds
- Ginger
- Lemon balm
- Lemon basil
- Lemongrass
- Lemon verbena (leaves and flowers)
- Mint (leaves and flowers)
- Rosemary
- Rose petals
- Sage
- Scented geranium (leaves and flowers)
- Sweet cicely
- Thyme
- Violet flowers

Makes about 2 cups

Years ago my maternal aunt, Noreen, showed me how she flavored granulated sugar by adding fresh vanilla beans brought back from a yearly trip home to the Caribbean. I have since experimented with a wide range of spices, herbs, and edible flowers and couldn't believe my eyes when I spotted jars of this simple treat for sale at a premium . . . after all, it's just sugar with a few herbs thrown in. Super easy to make. It makes a vibrant and exciting addition to baked goods, tea, coffee, sweet beverages, or anywhere else you use sugar.

1. Gently bruise the lavender buds in a mortar and pestle or with the back of a wooden spoon to release the aromatic oils.

2. Pour the blossoms and sugar into a clean Mason jar, shake vigorously, and store in a dark, dry place with the lid on.

NOTE: Store the lavender blossoms in the sugar indefinitely if you like. Pound or grind it lightly before use to release more flavor.

Leafy herbs such as scented geraniums and mint tend to turn brown and don't look very good over the long term. Sift the herbs out after about a week or so.

Freezing

Herbs that have been frozen can get a little mushy and will never be as good as they are fresh, straight off the plant. Though they may not be the ideal, frozen herbs aren't half bad and can last a long time if you know the trick to treating each herb. It's about the closest you can get to the real thing for long-term usage, and in the dead of winter, I'll take it.

Several herbs freeze exceptionally well with little fuss or bother. Lay flat whole stems of any of the herbs listed in the sidebar onto trays lined with parchment paper and set in the freezer for a few hours. Once frozen, break the leaves off the stems or transfer whole to freezer bags or freezable containers.

Basil and lemon balm need to be blanched first in order to prevent them from going black in the freezer. When putting up small batches, set the leaves in a fine-mesh sieve and pour boiling water over the top. Don't try to blanch by boiling in a pot or you'll cook the herb and lose all of that good flavor into the water. Squeeze out as much moisture as you can before packaging them up to freeze.

Herbal Ice Cubes

Herbs packed into convenient, individually sized servings have become the de rigueur way to keep popular herbs on hand year-round. I have to agree it works like a charm and keeps easily frozen herbs like parsley and lovage fresh for at least 6 months. I like to prepare a few batches of mixed herbs that we can pop into our favorite winter soups.

Freezing in Oil

Freezing with a bit of oil mixed in decreases the length of time an herb will stay fresh in the freezer, but significantly improves the flavor and texture of fussy herbs like basil that don't like to be frozen. The following pesto recipes can be frozen and kept in freezer bags or freezer-safe containers for a good 3 months or more, as long as you omit the cheese and reduce the salt content, because both ingredients impede proper freezing.

Herbs That Freeze Well
Bay
Chervil
Chives
Dill
Fennel
Garlic chives
Green onions
Lemongrass
Lemon verbena
Lovage
Marjoram
Mint
Oregano
Parsley
Rosemary
Sage
Tarragon
Thyme

Pesto and Pistou

Once you've grown your own herb garden, it's only a matter of time before you'll try your hand at making this famous Mediterranean sauce. All roads lead here. The conventional ingredients are basil, olive oil, and garlic, but the same basic principle can be applied to just about any herb in the garden.

Both *pesto* (the Italian version) and *pistou* (from the French Provençal) are traditionally pounded into a paste using a mortar and pestle. I urge you to try it this way if you're making a small batch and have the time to spare, as there is a profound difference from the electric processor version.

1. Place clean, dry herbs in a food processor or blender with oil, nuts, and/or garlic cloves (as each recipe indicates).

2. Pulse until the ingredients are blended and smooth. Using a knife, roughly chop tough, fibrous herbs such as sage and garlic scapes on their own before adding other ingredients.

3. Stir in Parmesan cheese and citrus juice by hand.

4. Add salt to taste.

Garlic Scape Pesto
Makes 1½ cups
There are lots of delicious ways to cook with garlic scapes, but if you grow only a handful, pesto is the only way to use it. Substitute tender green garlic for garlic scapes in the springtime.

12 garlic scapes, trimmed and roughly chopped

½ cup olive oil

1 cup grated Parmesan cheese

Juice of 1 lemon (or 2 tablespoons)

Sea salt to taste

Sage Pesto
Makes about ½ cup

1 cup (packed) sage leaves

½ cup olive oil

⅓ cup roasted walnuts

1 garlic clove

½ cup grated Parmesan cheese

1 tablespoon lemon juice

Sea salt to taste

My original plan for this pesto was as a topping for oven-baked squashes, but my spouse loves it and puts it on nearly everything.

Cilantro Pesto
Makes 1–1½ cups

1 shallot

¼–1 jalapeno pepper, roughly chopped, to taste

¼ cup pepitas, aka pumpkin seeds

2 cups (packed) cilantro leaves

Juice of 1 lime (or 2 tablespoons)

½ cup olive oil

Sea salt to taste

Whip up a batch of this Mexican-inspired pesto when your crop of cilantro bolts. Use it as a marinade or salsa topping for chicken, roasted vegetables, seafood, and tortillas. You can even cross cultures and spread some on a panini.

Mixed-Herb Coulis
Makes about ¾ cup

1 cup (packed) fresh parsley leaves

1 tablespoon fresh lemon thyme leaves

1 tablespoon roughly chopped fresh chives

1 tablespoon fresh tarragon leaves

1 tablespoon roughly chopped fresh sage

½ tablespoon fresh oregano leaves

½ cup olive oil

1 tablespoon lemon juice

Sea salt and pepper to taste

Despite the fancy name, this is really just a wet green sauce that you can drizzle on egg dishes or keep on hand for flavoring as you cook. Follow my recipe or make your own using the fresh herbs that are currently in abundance in your garden. Just about any combination works as long as you keep the ratio of powerful to mild herbs well proportioned.

Resources

Gardening Supplies
- Gardener's Supply Company (gardeners.com)
- Lee Valley (leevalley.com)
- Terrain at Styer's (shopterrain.com)

Organic Soils and Amendments
- Organic Mechanics (organicmechanicsoil.com)
- Natural Gardener (naturalgardeneraustin.com)
- Urban Harvest (uharvest.ca)

Seeds and Plants

UNITED STATES
- Botanical Interests (botanicalinterests.com)
- Bountiful Gardens (bountifulgardens.org)
- Johnny's Selected Seeds (johnnyseeds.com)
- Renee's Garden (reneesgarden.com)

CANADA
- Richters Herbs (richters.com)
- Seeds of Diversity Canada (seeds.ca)
- Solana Seeds (solanaseeds.netfirms.com)
- Urban Harvest (uharvest.ca)

UK
- Jekka's Herb Farm (jekkasherbfarm.com)

Find downloads and additional resources at easy-growing.com.

Acknowledgments

A whole lotta love to the many gardening geeks and geeks-to-be that I have met through YouGrowGirl.com over the years. Don't stop believing.

A promise of a vacation (soon, I swear) to Davin Risk, my best friend, partner (in all things), and amateur professional live-in barista. I truly could not have done any of this without your tireless support and enthusiasm, never mind all of the delicious coffees. It goes without saying that all of this is as much yours as it is mine. Team Trail-Risk!

Cheers to friends and gardening comrades Jennifer Parker, Sakurako Handa, Laura Berman, Gwynne Basen, Lorraine Johnson, Colette Murphy, Kelly Gilliam, Margaret Roach, Derek Powazek, Beate Schwirtlich, Coleen Vanderlinden, Meighan Makarchuk, Renee Garner, Julianna, and the elusive Mr. Brown Thumb.

Special thanks are due to patient friends with vehicles who have helped this nondriver schlep her plants around town and who have overindulged me with rides and day trips to out-of-town garden shops, greenhouses, nurseries, and gardens. I owe you: David Leeman, John Therrien, Melanie Roscoe, Laura Berman, and Brenda McCrank.

Thanks once again to a professional support system that has put a lot of faith in me and had my back through some tough moments: Laura Nolan, Sarah Sockit Moseley, Clarkson Potter, including Aliza Fogelson, Jane Treuhaft, Ada Yonenaka, Joan Denman, Peggy Paul, Emily Lavelle, and more.

Credits

Photography: Gayla Trail and Davin Risk; page 116 by Meighan Makarchuk

Illustrations: Davin Risk

Index

Note: page numbers in bold indicate the main discussion of a plant; page numbers in *italics* refer to photographs.